BRISTOL INTRODUCTIONS

The Language Connection

THOEMMES

ALSO IN THE SERIES

BERTRAND RUSSELL

by John Slater, *University of Toronto*

With a Preface by Ray Monk

PHILOSOPHY, MATHEMATICS, EDUCATION, POLITICS
ISBN 1 85506 347 6 : 184pp : Hb : 1994
ISBN 1 85506 346 8 : 184pp : Pb : 1994

PHILOSOPHY AND THE ARTS

by Andrew Harrison, *University of Bristol*

With a Preface by Ray Monk

PHILOSOPHY, ART THEORY
ISBN 1 85506 499 5 : c.180pp : Hb : 1996
ISBN 1 85506 500 2 : c.180pp : Pb : 1996

Printed in England by Antony Rowe

THE LANGUAGE CONNECTION

Philosophy and Linguistics

Roy Harris

Professor Emeritus of General Linguistics
University of Oxford

Preface by
Ray Monk

Series Editor
University of Southampton

THOEMMES PRESS

Published in 1996 by

Thoemmes Press
11 Great George Street
Bristol BS1 5RR
United Kingdom

ISBN 1 85506 497 9 – Hardback
ISBN 1 85506 498 7 – Paperback

British Library Cataloguing-in-Publication Data

A catalogue record of this title is available
from the British Library

CONTENTS

PREFACE

Among academics, an unfortunate tendency has grown up in recent years to contrast introductory books with those which 'make a contribution to the literature', as if one wrote either for one's peers or for the *hoi polloi*, but never both. In *The Language Connection*, Roy Harris has set his face against this tendency by writing a book that is, at one and the same time, an original contribution to current debates, *and* a stimulating introduction to its subject, readily intelligible to non-experts.

As the translator of Saussure, the author of several internationally acclaimed books on language (including *The Language Machine*, *The Language Myth*, and *The Origin of Writing*), and the Professor of General Linguistics at Oxford University, Roy Harris is supremely well-versed in 'the literature' on linguistics and the philosophy of language. But the purpose of this book is not to introduce his readers to that literature – in the bland and anodyne fashion that blights so many introductory texts – but rather to challenge its basic presuppositions. For two thousand years, Harris believes, language has been analysed by both philosophers and linguists from a point of view distorted by illusions and confusions, which both disciplines have had a vested interest in perpetuating, since they are precisely the illusions and confusions that provide the rationale for those disciplines.

Harris's aim is to examine what he calls the 'meta-linguistic framework' within which the study of language has been pursued by both philosophers and linguists since the days of the ancient Greeks. His view is that, despite appearances, it is essentially the *same* framework in both disciplines. To show this, he traces the parallel courses followed by, on the one hand, the grammarians (linguists) in their successive attempts to analyse the *sentence*, and, on the other, the logicians (philosophers) in their successive attempts to analyse the *proposition*. Both, Harris believes, were from the outset wild goose chases: neither the sentence, as conceived by the linguist, nor the proposition, as conceived by the philosopher, had anything other than a shadowy, theoretical existence. Each was equally a 'metalinguistic illusion', created by an unwarranted generalization from the 'reflexivity' that is a common feature of natural languages.

The reflexivity in question consists in the ability to use language to talk *about* language. Thus we ask of a thing 'What is that called?' and of a word 'What does that mean?'. In their proper context, Harris argues, these type of 'metalinguistic' questions are perfectly harmless. But when we attempt to ask, out of all specific contexts, what 'meaning' is, in general, we are in the grip of a metalinguistic illusion, one that *only* admits of illusory answers. As case studies, Harris subjects two of these illusory answers – one provided by the linguist, Leonard Bloomfield, and the other by the philosopher, A. J. Ayer – to a detailed scrutiny.

The division between the disciplines of philosophy and linguistics is, Harris maintains, artificial, and 'largely responsible for the failure so far in Western culture to deliver anything like a convincing account of language or a comprehensive rationale of linguistic investigation'. On this point, he is persuasive. But the question arises: supposing this division is overcome, and supposing the lessons Harris draws from the history of linguistic enquiry in the West were taken to heart – might there then be a *fruitful* investigation into language? Might there be such a thing as an 'adequate theory of language'? And, if so, what form would it take? Harris leaves these questions unanswered, beyond insisting that, whatever form it took, it would have to resist the temptation to study language out of context and would have to regard speech, not as a kind of 'machinery', but as 'a creative, interactive function of individuals'. Can one theorize without generalizing? Or can one imagine a form of inquiry into language that gives up theorizing altogether?

Of course, Harris's diagnosis of the malady at the centre of the Western tradition of linguistic investigations, raises as many questions as it answers. But that is as it should be. It is an introduction to the subject in the best possible sense: one that leaves its readers, not satisfied with having been given an answer to difficult problems, but engaged with those problems themselves, and with a better understanding of the difficulties they raise.

Ray Monk,
Southampton, 1996

INTRODUCTION

I would rather have my words stay fixed and stable than possess the wisdom of Daedalus and the wealth of Tantalus besides.

Socrates

'The question is,' said Alice, 'whether you *can* make words mean so many different things.'

Lewis Carroll

'I am embrangled in words,' writes Berkeley at one point in his notebook, evidently with some annoyance; but then adds immediately, as if by way of consolation, ''tis scarce possible it should be otherwise.'

Berkeley here speaks, if we are to be honest about it, for every philosopher who has ever lived. And, we might add, for every linguist too. Unfortunately, those in either discipline who have realized their own embranglement have been few, and those who admitted it with Berkeley's candour even fewer.

Only one philosopher of any note ever rejected the embranglement outright. That was Cratylus of Athens, who, according to legend, developed such a profound mistrust of language that he eventually renounced words altogether and communicated by means of gesture only. Presumably he thought that gestures were less risky than words. But it seems safe to say that if Cratylus' example had been universally followed, the disciplines we now call 'philosophy' and 'linguistics' would have been stifled at birth. For both are forms of inquiry which have an intrinsic engagement with language. Philosophical debate in a non-verbal mode is as difficult to imagine as a non-verbal linguistics. This shared dependence on words is one aspect of what we may call the 'language connection' between philosophy and linguistics.

By this term I mean to imply not merely that the embranglement of which Berkeley speaks is an occupational hazard for philosophers and linguists alike, nor even that philosophy and linguistics both have a professional interest in the elucidation of certain problems about language. I also mean that, at least in the Western tradition, neither of these two disciplines could have developed as it did without the other. There has been for many centuries either an overt or a tacit division of intellectual labour between the two; and that division has to do with language.

The connection I am referring to has a firm historical basis. Modern philosophy and modern linguistics both trace their antecedents back through a tradition of inquiry that began in the Classical period of ancient Greece. That connection was maintained throughout the Middle Ages, when logic, grammar and rhetoric were three basic components of the university curriculum – all three being concerned with aspects of language. The medieval *trivium* is still reflected in the organization of higher education right down to the present day, at least in Europe and America. Roughly speaking, the linguistic interests of modern philosophers fall in direct line of descent from the logicians of ancient and medieval times, while the concerns that dominate modern linguistics derive from the grammarians and, to some extent, from the rhetoricians.

A commonly held, but rather superficial, view sees

the respective domains of philosophy and linguistics as overlapping, rather than as interconnected at any deeper level. The linguist, on this view, is concerned with the study of language and nothing else; whereas for the philosopher, language is only one among many concerns. The very term 'philosophy of language' seems to imply as much. (Cf. 'philosophy of mind', 'philosophy of science', 'philosophy of education', etc.) And in a sense this is right. But at the same time it is misleading. For it disguises the fact that philosophy has to deal with certain linguistic problems in *all* its various branches of inquiry. The philosopher must, for instance, adopt a certain terminology appropriate to the particular field of investigation. The terms in question must be defined, the meanings of statements made within that field must be elucidated, and so on. And these are tasks which are no less 'linguistic' than those of the lexicographer or the grammarian.

On the other hand, it is equally superficial to suppose that the linguist's concern with language is merely observational and has no philosophical implications. Before linguistic 'facts' of any kind can be recorded or documented they must be established and identified. In short, a linguistic epistemology or theory of some kind must be in place, even if it is not overtly acknowledged as such. Frege once remarked that a thought is not something you can hand to an observer for examination, like a rock-crystal. But this goes too for words and all other units that the linguist qua linguist has any interest in.

At least since the time of Plato, philosophers have believed that language is intimately involved in human reasoning. Exactly how is controversial. Linguists, for their part, have presumed not merely to observe and describe linguistic phenomena but to reason about them and 'explain' them.

Thus where language is concerned both philosophy and linguistics have always to some extent shared a common technical vocabulary, and still do. For example, if you read what is currently published in English in philosophical and linguistic journals, you will find both philosophers and linguists using terms such as *word, sentence, form, meaning, subject, predicate, grammatical, ungrammatical, true, false, language, dialect,* and many more. (This does not mean they always see eye to eye with one another about the use of this vocabulary: far from it. But a connection which gives rise to contention is a connection all the same.)

What all this amounts to is that, far from following the example of Cratylus, philosophers and linguists in the Western tradition have always taken for granted that there is nothing paradoxical about using language as a tool for the rational description and investigation of language. Which is another way of saying that they accepted the notion that a fundamental potential of linguistic communication is reflexivity. It would have been odd indeed if they had denied that. For if language did not itself equip us to discuss language, then both philosopher and linguist would lack professional employment altogether.

To grasp this point, however, is to see that neither philosophy nor linguistics can lay claim to offering an entirely 'impartial' investigation of language and how it works. The language connection is not just a point of contact but a shared vested interest. The very ways in which philosophy and linguistics operate as disciplines would make it suicidal for either to deny the reflexivity of language. Thus there is *at least one* property of language which both must, in their own interests, accept and defend. Whether they give an adequate account of linguistic reflexivity is another matter: I shall argue that they fail in this.

According to Russell, Wittgenstein in the *Tractatus Logico-Philosophicus* held that it is impossible to speak about a language in the language itself. (Others, however, have doubted that this was Wittgenstein's position.) A more widely held view among philosophers is that languages provide us with all the requisite material for constructing metalanguages. And where this material comes from other than from the languages themselves it is difficult to see. In this sense at least, therefore, it seems that languages must be reflexive or potentially reflexive systems. That is, they can be extended in such a way as to allow discussion and analysis of their own constitution.

Such an extension, it seems to me, plays an essential role in the history of Western philosophy and Western linguistics. For it is hard to see how either of these inquiries can be said to have begun until a certain level of metalinguistic sophistication was reached. The point is obvious in the case of linguistics; to describe a word as a 'noun', a 'verb', an 'adverb', etc. is patently to impose a metalinguistic classification upon it. But although perhaps less obvious in the case of philosophy, the point is no less valid. Questions like 'What is virtue?' and 'What is justice?' are not philosophical questions because of being about virtue and justice (rather than about, say, income tax or the weather). What makes them philosophical questions is that we recognize an invitation to reflect on the use of a certain term or terms. The way such questions are formulated already suggests that we should take them as asking us to ponder, for example, 'What is it that is called *virtue*?', 'What is it that is called *justice*?', 'What kind of conduct is called *virtuous*?', 'What kind of act is called *just*?'. Or at least to *begin* by pondering such questions.

But that is not all. To take such questions seriously is already, albeit implicitly, to endorse certain assumptions about how language functions. Behind the question 'What is virtue?' lies the assumption that the words *virtue*, *virtuous*, etc. are not randomly applied to human behaviour, any more than the words *oak* and *ash* are randomly applied to trees. Otherwise there would be no point in raising the issue in that form in the first place.

Thus when I say that there is a 'language connection' between philosophy and linguistics in the Western tradition I am saying that there is a certain range of questions about language which neither discipline can afford to ignore. These questions are all concerned, in one way or another, with the kind of discourse which enables us to discuss language(s), and with the foundations on which such discourse is based. In short, they are metalinguistic questions.

The possibility of metalanguage is an important resource. For not all communication systems have this reflexive potential. It is often said to be one of the key features distinguishing (human) language from all forms of animal communication. Many species can communicate about the presence of predators; but none, as far as we know, can communicate about the signals which indicate that predators are present. They cannot propose, for example, that the presence of predators might be better indicated by a different signal.

Not all human communication systems have this reflexive potential built into them either. We are perfectly familiar, for instance, with traffic lights and the system of signals indicating 'stop', 'go', etc. But the messages this system can handle do not include any about the lights themselves. A proposal to let red mean 'go' and green mean 'stop' would have to be initiated – and debated – from outside.

Verbal messages, on the other hand, are not subject to any such limitation. We can and do – apparently – discuss words by citing them. We argue about what they mean. We advocate – or denounce – linguistic innovations. As Lewis Carroll once observed, there is nothing to stop anyone from proposing to use the word *black* to mean 'white' and the word *white* to mean 'black'. Or so both the philosopher and the linguist would have us believe. Not that they often advance such iconoclastic proposals. But without the underpinning of reflexivity, neither the philosopher's discussion of the meanings of such words as *good*, *virtue*, and *beauty*, nor the linguist's analysis of their phonology and grammar, would make much sense at all.

But do the philosopher and the linguist fully understand what linguistic reflexivity involves? Might not the reflexivity they take for granted be an illusion? Or a carefully doctored version designed for their own disciplinary purposes? These sceptical questions are the point of departure for the discussion presented in the following chapters. In the search for answers, it will be necessary to subject some of the most basic terms in our metalinguistic vocabulary to a more critical scrutiny than either philosophers or linguists usually give them. And the effect of this will be to put the whole relationship between philosophy and linguistics, together with their common dependence on language, in an unaccustomed and perhaps unwelcome perspective. We might even come to see that Berkeley's resignation to verbal embranglement was not despair and Cratylus' mistrust of words not quite as absurd as it is usually thought to be.

Clearly, it has been in the professional interest of both disciplines *as disciplines* to play down the extent of their own embranglement, or else to claim that the dangers have been seen and successfully surmounted. Whether this can be claimed today with any greater confidence than in the past is another question.

In case there may be any residual doubt lingering in the reader's mind, let me make it clear that this book is not intended to be read as a history – or even a historical survey – of the views that Western philosophers and linguists have held about language. (For a detailed comparison of the positions of one very influential linguist and one very influential philosopher, see my book *Language, Saussure and Wittgenstein*, London, Routledge, 1988.) Nevertheless, my argument appeals to historical considerations at certain crucial points. My aim is to focus on how Western philosophy and linguistics set up – and attempt to regiment – discourse about language.

In his autobiography, Leonard Woolf speaks of 'the purification of that divinely cathartic question which echoed through the Cambridge courts of my youth as it had 2300 years before echoed through the streets of Socratic Athens.' The question, says Woolf, was: 'What do you mean by that?'. My method will be to try to use that 'divinely cathartic question' – a metalinguistic question if ever there was one – as a way of probing Western metalinguistic discourse itself. I hope that the ancient powers of purification are not yet exhausted.

*   *   *

Since the issues discussed in this book turn very largely on the use of technical terms by philosophers and linguists, it is difficult to avoid them. However, I have tried to discuss these technical terms in as non-technical a way as possible. In so doing, I am aware of having occasionally cut theoretical corners in a provocative manner. But since the provocations in these cases are no greater than those I offer when not corner-cutting, and part of my brief was to write a fairly short book, I have not burdened the discussion by drawing the reader's attention to the niceties involved.

Finally, I would like to thank Peter Hacker and Justin Gosling for finding the time to look at earlier versions of some of the chapters, and Rita Harris for reading and correcting the final draft.

Chapter 1
QUESTIONS ABOUT LANGUAGE

'What is the definition of the word *entropy*?' 'Did she say *trip* or *drip*?' 'How do you spell [fiziks]?' 'What is the subject of the sentence *Ice melts*?' 'How do you say "Good morning" in Spanish?'

All these are metalinguistic questions. The first point to note about them is that if we could not ask such questions, neither philosophy nor linguistics, as currently practised, could even get started. I invite the reader to imagine what the consequences would be for both disciplines if metalinguistic questions were suddenly banned from respectable academic discourse. The effect would be as devastating as banning questions about the stars from astronomy.

The second point to note is that philosophy and linguistics do not have any monopoly of metalinguistic questions. Such questions can be – and often are – asked by all kinds of people going about their everyday linguistic affairs. As lay questions they are perfectly sensible and (usually) get sensible answers. However, as construed by philosophers and linguists, it is far from clear that they are sensible questions at all. Both disciplines trade on our lay linguistic assumptions, but in the case of metalinguistic questions – I am suggesting – the way they do so is meretricious and self-serving. It throws no light at all on our lay linguistic experience.

So what does it mean to put such questions as the above into the 'metalinguistic' category? What it means,

1

according to many theorists, is that we understand these questions as asking something about words or combinations of words. Therefore such questions would not make much sense if we could not pick out some unit in the interrogative formulation itself which served to identify the word or words in question.

This, it should be noted, is a quite different matter from asking a further question: can the word or words actually be identified? The working assumption, doubtless, is that they can be. For it would be silly or else misguided to ask for the definition of *entropy* if there is no such word, or for the subject of *Ice melts* if there is no such sentence or no such subject.

It is also a different matter from asking *how* the word(s) in question are presented to us in the interrogative formulation. In this chapter, the examples under discussion are all presented in written form. This presupposes an acquaintance with – in this instance – the Roman alphabet and graphic devices such as full stops, inverted commas, question marks and italicization.

Let us set these two further questions aside for the moment in order to focus on the first issue – that of metalinguistic reference. For if we cannot sort that problem out in some satisfactory way, the other questions are either nonsensical or else, at least, badly put. We first need to know, in short, how to make sense of the general notion that a language – call it L (in this case English) – in either its spoken or written form enables us to discuss its own properties and functions (i.e. those of L), including the elements of which it is constituted (e.g. the words of L) and instances of their use (e.g. utterances or inscriptions in L).

Both philosophy and linguistics are inquiries nowadays often conducted in such a manner as to assume that sense can indeed be made of this general notion. According to a recent and rather bland reassurance by one linguist,

> it is a commonplace of philosophical semantics that natural languages (in contrast with many non-natural, or artificial, formal languages) contain their own metalanguage: they may be used to describe, not only other languages (and language in general), but also themselves.[1]

Even more blandly, the same author goes on to say that 'philosophical problems that can be caused by this kind of reflexivity will not be of direct concern to us here'. In other words, linguistics is in the clear. But is it? If the accepted 'commonplace' should itself prove to be a mistake, it is difficult to avoid the conclusion that neither philosophers nor linguists understand what they are doing when they formulate questions metalinguistically. That would not only be a disaster for the writer of the textbook quoted above: it would be something of a blow to the claims of both disciplines.

*   *   *

Before proceeding further, it should be pointed out that the term *metalanguage* itself is not always used in exactly the same way by philosophers and linguists. For instance, I find the following explanations given in *The Encyclopedia of Philosophy* (New York, Macmillan, 1967) under the entry 'Glossary of logical terms' (vol. 5, pp. 57–77):

---

[1] J. Lyons, *Linguistic Semantics: An Introduction*, Cambridge, Cambridge University Press, 1995, p. 7.

metalanguage. A language used to talk about an object language; a *meta-metalanguage* is a language used to talk about a metalanguage, and so forth. Derivatively, a proposition is said to be in the metalanguage if and only if it is about an expression in the object language.

object language. A language used to talk about things, rather than about other languages. Derivatively, a proposition is said to be in the object language if and only if it is not about any linguistic expression. "Socrates was a philosopher" is therefore in the object language, whereas "'Socrates' has eight letters" is not.

I note in passing that this glossary nowhere defines the expression *a language*. Thus straight away the philosopher is trading on the assumption that lay people and specialists alike all understand what a language is. From a lay point of view, unfortunately, this assumption immediately generates a puzzle. For both "Socrates was a philosopher" and "'Socrates' has eight letters" clearly belong to the same language, viz. English. But the definitions say nothing about the possibility of an object language containing its own metalanguage, and thus being used to talk about itself. However, let us not quibble yet with the philosopher's definition of *metalanguage*, but simply compare it with the following gloss provided by a linguist (D. Crystal, *Encyclopedic Dictionary of Language and Languages*, Oxford, Blackwell, 1992, p. 249):

metalanguage. A language for describing an object of study, such as the technical language of chemistry, engineering or law. The headwords in the present book constitute a linguistic metalanguage.

This entry is no less puzzling in its own way, but certainly gives us a rather different account of what a metalanguage is. It is puzzling because one finds it hard to understand how a simple list of terms, such as the headwords in a dictionary, constitutes a language (whether meta- or not). For a language is more than its lexicon: to call such a list a language is rather like calling a collection of coins a currency. Furthermore, on this definition *Lanthanum belongs to group IIIb of the periodic table* is clearly a metalinguistic formulation, whereas according to the philosopher's definition it is not.

However, whether we take the philosopher's definition or the linguist's, the term *metalanguage* itself counts as a metalinguistic (or, if anyone insists, meta-metalinguistic) term; and there is no reason to suppose that such terms are somehow immune from the problems of definition that beset other terms. Nowhere in language can we expect to find a definitional bedrock on which to build unproblematic metalanguages or other types of verbal and notational system. To imagine otherwise would be an illusion (quite apart from being bad linguistics and bad philosophy). And this brings us back again immediately to the question of making sense of the general notion of linguistic reflexivity.[2]

* * *

I wish to argue that the two most commonly accepted academic strategies for making sense of this general notion are both irreparably flawed. These two strategies

[2] Children's acquisition of metalanguage is now a flourishing field of research. See J. E. Gombert, *Metalinguistic Development*, Chicago, University of Chicago Press, 1992.

rely on what I shall call (i) the doctrine of use and mention, and (ii) the doctrine of types and tokens. They are closely related.

The doctrine of use and mention begins by drawing our attention to the difference between two ways in which words appear to function in everyday discourse. For example, the reply 'John' might be given either in answer to such a question as 'Who are we waiting for?' or in answer to the question 'What's your name?'. Similarly, the reply 'John has pneumonia' might be given either in answer to such a question as 'What is John suffering from?' or in answer to a question such as 'What is that sentence on the blackboard?'. Philosophers of an earlier age invented technical terms for drawing this distinction. They spoke of *suppositio formalis* and *suppositio materialis*. Thus there were two distinct meanings associated with a supposedly ambiguous statement such as 'John is monosyllabic'. In one case this was interpreted as saying that John expresses himself in words of one syllable (*suppositio formalis*). In the other case (*suppositio materialis*) it was interpreted as a statement about the word *John*, i.e. that it consists of a single syllable. This was regarded as an important distinction, for on one interpretation we might be dealing with a true assertion but on the other interpretation with a false assertion. It is at this point that the doctrine of use and mention ties in with the philosopher's traditional concern for distinguishing between truth and falsity.

Questions of truth and falsity are also metalinguistic questions. That is to say, when we ask 'Is that true?' we are usually asking about what someone has said or written. Or else we are asking about what someone might say or write. In short, to make sense of such a question we have to relate it, explicitly or implicitly, to a verbal formulation of some kind. However, when we say 'That is true' in response to what someone said, it is often far from clear whether it is a case of *suppositio formalis* or *suppositio materialis*. (Are we endorsing the words used, or the sentiment expressed? Or both?) The issue is complicated by the fact that we are all familiar with an everyday linguistic procedure which allows reports of direct speech (*oratio recta*) to be reformulated as indirect speech (*oratio obliqua*). Thus *John said 'I don't smoke'* becomes *John said he didn't smoke*. In the latter formulation we have lost the overt citation of John's actual words, although in some sense they seem to be still present. Similarly with *'Red is a colour' is true* and *It is true that red is a colour*.

Why were the terms *suppositio formalis* and *suppositio materialis* originally chosen? This relates to an ancient distinction between form and substance and to theories of the 'properties of terms' in medieval times. Although I think that the ghost of the ancient distinction still lurks behind the modern doctrine of use and mention, I do not pursue the matter further here. It is irrelevant to the main objection I wish to lodge against the doctrine in its modern form.

The modern way of restating the difference between *suppositio formalis* and *suppositio materialis* is this. When 'John is monosyllabic' is taken as saying something about the way John speaks we have a *use* of the name *John*. When it is taken as saying something about the name, we have a *mention* of the name. In the former case, it is the person himself who is mentioned, by using his name.

It is often recommended that in writing it is advisable to avoid possible confusion by employing such devices as inverted commas and italics. ('"John" is monosyllabic' [= mention of the name] vs. 'John is monosyllabic'

[= use of the name].) Exactly how this distinction is rendered graphically, we are told, does not greatly matter (we could, for instance, choose to put the name in red to indicate mention) provided that it is indicated somehow or other. How to indicate it orally in a parallel manner is rather more problematic. But the problem is not in theory insuperable. (For instance, we could adopt the convention of pronouncing the name an octave higher than usual in order to signal occasions of mention. The fact that no spoken language in the world that has so far been studied adopts any such expedient is, I am inclined to think, not without significance; but for the moment we may ignore it.)

To summarize thus far, the doctrine of use and mention appears to provide a sound basis for validating the idea that we need to pay attention to a subtlety of everyday usage that might otherwise confound our best efforts to clarify the problem. This subtlety is, supposedly, of quite general scope; that is to say, *any* given word, phrase, sentence, etc. may be either used or mentioned. And it has an important bearing on issues of truth and falsity to determine, in any given instance, which is the case. Thus, allegedly, we are dealing not with a distinction peculiar to this language or that, or to certain forms of argument only, but with a universal property of language in general. Furthermore, it is in virtue of this property that philosophers, linguists and others can (i) give meaningful and accurate verbal descriptions of particular words, phrases, sentences, etc., and (ii) deploy these descriptions in the systematic investigation of other properties and functions of language and languages.

The doctrine of use and mention is put to work in contemporary philosophy and linguistics in all kinds of ways. An exhaustive survey would occupy many more pages than are contained in this book. Two typical examples must here suffice to indicate how important the doctrine is to both disciplines.

From philosophy let us take what is sometimes known as the 'semantic conception' of truth. According to Tarski, who introduced this notion, the following formula captures the type of equivalence to which an adequate definition of truth must conform: *The sentence "snow is white" is true if, and only if, snow is white.*[3] The point to note here is that, whether we agree with the 'semantic conception' of truth or not, its very formulation makes no sense unless we already accept the viability of the metalinguistic doctrine of use and mention. Tarski obviously does accept it, not only in the formula itself but in his explanation of what it (allegedly) means. He claims that here we have two occurrences of the same phrase (*snow is white*), once in what he calls 'quotation marks' and once without. (What exactly is being quoted here he never explains.) What appears in 'quotation marks' he describes as the 'name' of the sentence, while on the right-hand side of the equation, without these marks, appears 'the sentence itself'. Thus the formula (sc. of the form ["X" is true if and only if X]), on this interpretation, says something about a particular sentence, the sentence in question being identified not by using it but by mentioning it.

From linguistics, let us take a traditional grammarian's statement such as '*tristis* is a third-declension adjective' or 'the plural of *boy* is *boys*'. According to the doctrine of use and mention, here *tristis, boy* and *boys* are names of words, or names of forms. These names are here

---

[3] A. Tarski, 'The semantic conception of truth', *Philosophy and Phenomenological Research*, vol. 4, 1944, pp. 341–75. Reprinted in L. Linsky (ed.), *Semantics and the Philosophy of Language*, Urbana, University of Illinois Press, 1952.

being used in order to say something about the grammatical behaviour of the corresponding words or forms mentioned. (It should be noted, however, that as a 'word' *tristis* is not on a par with *boy* and *boys*. The latter are sometimes distinguished by called them 'word forms', of which *tristis* itself has a number, e.g. *triste, tristes. Boy* and *boys*, on the other hand, would both be word forms of the word *boy*.) A grammar of the traditional kind is to be interpreted as a compendium of such statements, all based on the distinction between use and mention.

The doctrine of types and tokens, which we owe in its modern form to C. S. Peirce, draws a related distinction in a somewhat different manner. Peirce begins by drawing our attention to two different ways of counting words.[4] One is the way in which printers count words when determining the length of a text. Here each occurrence of, say, *John* counts as a separate word: there may be twenty of them or more on a single page. But according to the other way of counting, all these would be examples of a single word, i.e. the name *John*, and it would make no difference whether there were just one individual or more than one so named. Similarly, in *Boys will be boys* we have on the first method of reckoning a sentence of four words, but on the second method of reckoning only three, since the single word *boys* occurs twice. (Peirce does not here acknowledge the distinction between words and word forms.) Peirce called the items counted by the printer *tokens*, and the units counted when we disregard multiple occurrences of these items *types*. All tokens, according to this view, will be tokens of a certain type, and the type in question

---

[4] C. S. Peirce, *Collected Papers*, ed. C. Hartshorne and P. Weiss, Cambridge, Mass., Harvard University Press, vol. IV, 1933, §537.

may have many – potentially an infinite number of – tokens. (This distinction may be applied not only to words, but to parts of words, single letters, phrases, sentences, etc.)

Again, the type-token distinction may be invoked, either explicitly or implicitly, in very many ways both in philosophy and in linguistics. For example, philosophers often warn us that we should pay attention to a number of different uses or meanings of the word *good*, or the word *true*. This advice may be interpreted as implicitly appealing to the notion that we are dealing with a single type (the English word *good*, or *true*) of which different tokens may be differently employed in different contexts. Similarly with the lexicographer who lists in the dictionary a single entry for *good* or *true*, but distinguishes under that entry a number of different meanings. This way of presenting the matter may likewise be interpreted as presupposing that there is a single type, which different authors or speakers constantly use, thus producing a multiplicity of tokens. The dictionary is often regarded as the model Peirce had in mind when introducing his distinction. (Thus the lexicographer's lemma or headword in the entry is what identifies the lexical type. Any examples quoted to illustrate the use of the word provide, accordingly, tokens of this type.)

For purposes of my argument, I do not need to show in detail how crippling it would be both for philosophy and for linguistics if these disciplines were deprived of the kinds of assumptions and the kinds of arguments that rest on these doctrines. I assume that this will already be obvious to the reader. Both doctrines presuppose that linguistic units of some kind (whether they are called *words*, *sentences*, or anything else does not greatly matter) are available for verbal – i.e. metalinguistic – identification. If these units – whatever we call them and however we define them – cannot be thus identified, then all arguments based upon that assumption immediately collapse. And that collapse, I venture to think, would undermine the foundations of both disciplines in their current mode. (And, for that matter, in the mode they and their precursors have adopted throughout two millenia of intellectual history in the West.) For it would deprive both philosophers and linguists of their chosen metalanguage.

*   *   *

The second phase in my argument is to show that the doctrine of use and mention and the doctrine of types and tokens, although not identical in content, are in fact versions – or aspects, if you prefer – of the same basic approach to language. This approach I call 'segregational'.

The term *segregational* is chosen to reflect the notion that communication systems, including languages like English, exist independently not only of one another but of how they may – or may not – be used by those who use them. On this view, there are two segregated domains of inquiry. One of these encompasses questions about the communication system(s) as such. The other encompasses questions about particular uses and users. These two domains, it is usually maintained, are related. Nevertheless, they are in principle separate, and for the segregationist it is a basic epistemological error to think that questions about the system can be reduced to questions about its use or its users.

Segregational thinking has dominated modern linguistics and modern philosophy. This is no coincidence. For segregational thinking and segregational terminology are admirably suited to the academic politics of both disciplines. To the outside world, the linguist and the philosopher wish to present themselves professionally as authorities in charge of certain areas of investigation. For that is how academic disciplines are justified (and financed). Thus just as the physicist is the expert whose domain is physics, and the chemist the expert whose domain is chemistry, so it has to be plausible for both linguist and philosopher to identify specific domains in which their professional expertise is exercised. The problem is that it is hard to identify these latter domains in any straightforward way. That is where a segregational rhetoric comes in handy. By treating – and constantly referring to – words, sentences, etc. as linguistic objects existing in their own right, it becomes possible to create the impression – and to convince oneself – that these objects provide materials for scientific investigation, just as physical objects do for the physicist and chemical substances do for the chemist.

Both the doctrine of use and mention and the doctrine of types and tokens are characteristic products of segregational thinking about language. Neither would hold water without the assumption that a legitimate – and inevitable – first step in linguistic investigation is to see speech and writing as involving the recurrent instantiation of a given set of units of various kinds. The doctrine of use and mention supports this by reifying the units. It also claims that we have available a universal technique for identifying these units for purposes of discussion: this universal technique is based on creating 'names' for them. (In some magical way, it is supposed that inverted commas, italicization and other graphic procedures can bring into existence written names for whatever forms are subjected to these procedures.) The doctrine of types and tokens likewise supports the recognition of an identifiable set of units, by proposing that we adopt another universally available technique: this involves classification. Specifically, the classification recommended is that of treating all particular items in a class as concrete manifestations (audible or visible) of a corresponding abstraction. The abstraction is not to be equated or identified with any of its manifestations, although, in a mysterious way not fully explained, the type is somehow embodied in each and every one of its tokens and is accordingly recognizable as such. (Thus *snow is white* and *snow is white* are, without further ado, deemed to be recognizable as tokens of the same type.)

Both doctrines, I suggest, are implausible metaphysical speculations. On the printed page, their implausibility is disguised (on first inspection) merely by the fact that we are familiar with certain conventions of writing. Thus it does not immediately strike us that there is anything suspicious about the general notion that two identically spelt forms are in some sense 'the same' linguistic unit. Nor about the general notion that, by applying some agreed graphic procedure, we can create 'names' of expressions at will. But both assumptions lend powerful support to the segregational view which insists that 'the language' (its words, sentences, etc.) is one thing and what people do with it (or with them) is another.

*   *   *

Why do I reject both the doctrine of use and mention and the doctrine of types and tokens? I shall give a more detailed answer in a later chapter. Why do I postpone the answer? In order, in the intervening chapters, to examine certain other metalinguistic doctrines which connect with and support the two doctrines I reject. In this way, I hope to show that we are dealing here with an interlocking structure of assumptions about how language works, and my strategy will be to urge that if major doctrinal props in that structure are withdrawn, then the whole must collapse.

However, to anticipate, one reason why I reject both the use-and-mention doctrine and the types-and-tokens doctrine is that neither honestly faces the question of *what*, exactly, we are supposed to be distinguishing *between*. It seems to me radically unclear how we can make sense of such implications as the following: (i) that every linguistic unit or event has – or can be given – a 'name'; (ii) that such 'names' are automatically conjured into existence by the operation of selected graphic devices, (iii) that we cannot speak or write except by producing utterances or inscriptions that *re*produce prior abstractions of some kind, and (iv) that it is somehow open to inspection or intuition which particular abstract units are involved in the day-to-day business of speaking and writing.

Thus, at best, the doctrines I am rejecting merely postpone all the crucial questions. Far from explaining how, in linguistic communication, the postulated system is related to the verbal operations we engage in, these doctrines take that relationship for granted. At worst, by dodging the issue, they introduce a pervasive confusion into all discussions of language.

I am willing to entertain the 'best' scenario; but I suspect that in practice we are almost always dealing with the 'worst'. The reason why I suspect the latter is that it is just too convenient for philosophers and linguists to invoke these theoretical doctrines in order to justify their own traditional practices. Here history enters into the picture. It would be naive to suppose that modern philosophy or modern linguistics dropped suddenly into university curricula out of a clear blue sky. That is why I now turn to considerations of a historical nature. These considerations concern the origins of some of the metalinguistic questions which philosophers and linguists purport to deal with.

Chapter 2
SPEECH AND ITS PARTS

Western metalinguistics got off to a disastrous start in Athens in the fourth century BC. It has never quite recovered.

Greek thinkers of that period, for various reasons, were not content to treat language as an activity *sui generis*. The intellectual history of the Western world might have been very different if they had. They saw language merely as one facet of *logos*, the mental faculty which supposedly distinguished human beings from the rest of the animal kingdom. Speech, as far as they were concerned, was first and foremost an external manifestation of *logos*.

It would be difficult to exaggerate how profoundly this initial assumption moulded all discussion of language which derives directly or indirectly from Greek sources.

English grammarians today still talk of 'parts of speech' and French grammarians of *parties du discours*. Both terms are ultimately translations of the Greek *meros logou* (Latin *pars orationis*). The Greek notion seems to have been that speech (= *logos* in its verbal manifestation), like everything else in the world, must be divisible. Atomism – if that is the appropriate term to use – was such a pervasive feature of Greek thinking about the world that it probably never occurred to any Greek to ask exactly what sense it makes to start linguistic inquiry from the assumption that speech is made up of 'parts'. But once that assumption had been made, there immediately emerged the task of identifying the 'parts' thus postulated and so answering the question 'How many parts are there?'.

What we see very early in the Western tradition is the development of two somewhat divergent attempts to map the notion of 'parts' of speech on to a basic metalinguistic framework which pictures speech as the process by which information is conveyed from *A* to *B*, or vice versa. Words are 'instruments of teaching', according to Socrates in Plato's *Cratylus*: their communicational function is to inform.

But where does this notion of 'parts' itself come from? Etymologists rush in where angels fear to tread. They will point out that there is a Greek word *merops*, found already in Homer, which presumably means something like 'dividing' and is used as a commonplace epithet to differentiate the human being from other creatures. In other words, having *logos* is associated at a very early date with dividing (= articulating) the sounds you produce. Animal cries are 'inarticulate' (= undivided). Human beings (*meropes brotoi*) are thus distinguished by dividing the noises they make.

One etymological guess (the phrase is tautological, since all etymology is guesswork) might be that what happened in Greece was that a distinction originally applied to the mechanism of sound production was transferred – in the human case – to what the vocal sound produced, i.e. speech.

Some support for this suggestion might be seen in the following fact. When Aristotle discusses the general notion of quantity (*Categories* VI) and draws a basic distinction between discrete and continuous quantity, the two examples he gives of the former are number and speech. It is hard to imagine that a modern theorist would have chosen the second example, and the way

Aristotle pairs the two is revealing. He proceeds to demonstrate that number is discontinuous by pointing out that when two fives make ten, there is no overlap or merging between the items added. (Otherwise, presumably, they would make less than ten.) The fact that speech is quantitative in nature he says is evident from the fact that it is measured in long and short syllables. The syllables do not overlap or merge either. (Otherwise, presumably, the metrical count in Greek verse would not work.) Hence speech is quantitatively discontinuous.

Whatever we may think of this argument, it throws some light on the original Greek notion of the divisibility of speech, which is clearly related to poetic practice. In view of the insistence by modern theorists on the 'linearity' of speech (see Chapter 3), it is interesting to note in passing that Aristotle's first example of *non*-discrete quantity is the (geometrical) line.

Evidently, there is some kind of analogy, but also a serious gap, between the notion that the spoken utterance divides into phonetically discrete parts (= syllables? sounds?) and the notion that *what is said* also divides into discrete parts. It is the latter that underlies the grammatical doctrine of the parts of speech.

The account scholars give us of the history of the Greek parts of speech goes rather like the song about the ten green bottles, but in reverse. Originally, it seems there were only two parts of speech (the minimum, since recognizing only one would have been self-contradictory) but this meagre number was soon increased to three by adding a ragbag category to take care of parts that did not fit easily into either of the first two. Later, the Stoics got as far as five. By the time we come to the first extant grammatical treatise from the Greek world, traditionally dated to about the second century BC and attributed to Dionysius Thrax, the number had risen to eight.[1] It was to stay at about that tally for many centuries to come.

Let us assume that this story is roughly right, and proceed to ask what exactly it meant – for the Greeks – to make the metalinguistic claim that there were two, or eight, or fifty-nine 'parts of speech'?

The question is difficult for a variety of reasons, not least because the Greeks do not seem to have had a very clear idea themselves of the sense in which *logos* has 'parts'. The usual modern interpretation of the phrase 'parts of speech' is to construe it in terms of word classes. (Thus *man, horse, water* are said to fall under the part of speech called 'noun', *tall, swift* and *wet* under the part of speech called 'adjective', etc.) But it would be anachronistic to foist this view retrospectively on to philosophers of the fourth century BC. For them the essential parts of speech were *onoma* and *rhema*, often misleadingly translated as 'noun' and 'verb'. A less misleading translation might be 'subject' and 'predicate', were it not that these are nowadays terms which already presuppose a level of analysis distinct from that at which 'parts of speech' are located.

The conceptual problem here is that discussion of language in the earliest period of Greek philosophical inquiry had not got as far as drawing even the crudest distinctions which all modern theorists take for granted. We are dealing with a metalanguage in the making, where no one has yet thought very hard about systematizing ways of talking about speech.

It is doubtful, for instance, whether even Aristotle distinguished clearly between the metalinguistic and the non-metalinguistic uses of words. Kneale and Kneale

---

[1]   J. Lallot, *La Grammaire de Denys le Thrace*, Paris: CNRS, 1989.

cite Aristotle's puzzling statement (*Categories* V) that 'man is predicated of a subject, the individual man, but is present in no subject' and suggest that Aristotle was simply unaware of the ambiguity which renders this obscure to modern scholars.

> He had almost certainly not asked himself the question, 'Does the sign *anthropos* (in the original of the sentence quoted above) stand for the Greek word *anthropos* or for some extra-linguistic entity? He lacked two devices which later logicians and philosophers have found indispensable in making their points clear, inverted commas and the free invention of abstract nouns. We can ask ourselves, 'Is Aristotle saying that "man" is predicated of the individual or that humanity is predicated of the individual?'. But Aristotle had only one sign, namely, *anthropos* to do duty for the three English signs, 'man', 'the word "man"', and 'humanity'.[2]

The implications of this statement are worth dwelling on for a moment. Three interesting points arise. 1. If Kneale and Kneale are right, the position is even more complicated than their description suggests. That is, Aristotle's statement in *Categories* V conflates not two but at least three possible claims: (i) a grammatical claim to the effect that the word *anthropos* can be used predicatively of individuals, (ii) a semantic claim to the effect that when this word is thus used the individual is assigned to a certain class of beings, and (iii) a logical claim to the effect that when such an assignment is made by using the word thus, then humanity is being predicated of the individual. 2. It is not altogether clear

[2] W. Kneale and M. Kneale, *The Development of Logic*, rev. ed., Oxford, Clarendon, 1984, pp. 26–7.

whether Kneale and Kneale are suggesting (i) that Aristotle *was* clear about all this, but simply could not express it clearly for lack of a developed metalanguage, or (ii) that lack of a developed metalanguage *prevented* Aristotle (and presumably other thinkers) from grasping these distinctions. 3. After discussing the problem of interpretation, Kneale and Kneale come to the conclusion that although Aristotle was not aware of the ambiguity, if he had been he would have declared himself to be talking about things not words. It is difficult to know whether we are supposed to interpret this conclusion simply as a denial of 2 (i), or as an attempt to award Aristotle an anachronistic accolade as a thinker. (Cf. If Caesar had had heavy artillery, he would have used it against the Gauls.) It makes little sense even to ask the question 'Did X mean *p* or *q*?' if the distinction between *p* and *q* is assumed to be beyond X's grasp.

The possible confusions involved in imposing modern metalinguistic questions retrospectively on the logicians and grammarians of antiquity are an ever-present risk in this kind of discussion, and that risk must constantly be borne in mind in this and the following chapters. Nevertheless, as should be evident from what has been said already, there is no way of avoiding it entirely except by renouncing any attempt to investigate the metalinguistics underlying what ancient authorities say. With this caveat, let us venture on the elucidation of some elementary distinctions concerning the 'parts of speech'.

The original distinction between *onoma* and *rhema* seems to have been based on nothing more subtle than the thought that *A* talks to *B* in order to say something specific, and that in order to say something about anything (and to be understood as having said it) at least two requirements have to be satisfied. The first requirement is to identify *who* or *what* it is you are talking about. The second is to attribute some state or action or property to the person(s) or thing(s) thus identified. You have to do this, for example, if you want to say of Socrates that he is asleep, or coughing, or very old; or of democracy that it is a good thing or a bad thing.

From this first assumption it is but a short step to supposing that language therefore has to supply us, at the very least, with two separate verbal tools for these two kinds of purpose. As already noted above, the metaphor of tools or instruments appears very early on in philosophical discussions of language. We find it likened to a weaver's shuttle: it is an instrument for separating or dividing reality.[3] Here again the emphasis is on segmenting a whole into its parts. Thus the name *Socrates*, for example, comes to be seen as an instrument by means of which the *logos* separates reality into just two parts: one part consisting of the individual thus named, and the rest consisting of everything else that is not-Socrates.

What is already happening here, clearly enough, is that speech is being separated into 'parts' on the basis of its supposed functions. The bi-partite division of a minimal statement into (i) *onoma* and (ii) *rhema* is no more than a reflection of the bi-partite division of what the utterance tells us. Roughly, it 'rhematizes' about what it has 'onomatized'.

It is remarkable how long in Western thinking about language this simple-minded analysis survived unchallenged. In the second half of the twentieth century, undergraduates in linguistics courses were still being

---

[3] Plato, *Cratylus*, 388.

taught as gospel that every sentence, however many words it may contain, divides by nature into NP + VP, where NP stands for 'noun phrase' and VP stands for 'verb phrase'. (If there happened to be no noun phrase at all, as in *Shut up!* or *Yes, please*, the story students were told was that it was 'really' there underneath the surface of the sentence all the time, but was simply invisible and/or inaudible. 'Deep structure' thus became a haven for all the unobservable Platonic entities that linguistic theorists wanted to postulate.) The initial phase of modern transformational-generative grammar could in fact be regarded as an elaborately formalized apologia for the original Greek division into *onoma* and *rhema*. But whereas the Greeks were modestly proposing no more than an account of Greek, the transformational grammarians more than two millennia later were claiming that the same basic analysis applied to all languages, however superficially disparate they might appear.

In the interim, a great deal had happened both in philosophy and in grammar, but the parts-of-speech doctrine survived all cataclysms more or less unscathed. It is interesting to inquire how and why. One clue is that even the severest critics of the traditional parts-of-speech doctrine found themselves at a loss to provide any more convenient basis for comparing one language with another. In others words, what I am suggesting is that the doctrine and its terminology came to provide an indispensable link between theoretical generalizations about language and common educational practice. One example among many that could be cited I take from a transformational grammarian of the 1960s. He condemns the traditional parts-of-speech doctrine as projecting:

a picture of language structure based on an inadequate logic, a confusion between logic and linguistics,
and a set of categories derived through Latin from the
Greek grammarians.[4]

Nevertheless, in the same work he protests:

> The differences between languages have been stressed
> so much in recent years that we tend to overlook the
> very real similarities. It is quite true that "verb" does
> not mean the same thing (in terms of categories of
> inflection, and so on) in discussing, say, Japanese
> grammar and English grammar. On the other hand,
> it is just as true that Japanese verbs parallel English
> verbs in many ways, and there is no need to apologize
> for calling both classes by the same name.[5]

In fact his book, *An Introduction to Transformational
Grammars*, makes extensive use of such traditional
parts-of-speech terms as *noun*, *verb*, *adjective*, *article*
and *adverb*, which are treated as being entirely
perspicuous. The grammarian's dilemma is obvious.
He tries to dismiss it by saying there 'is no need to
apologize' for what he is doing. But it is not a question
of anyone wanting him to apologize. Nor is it merely
a question, as he tries to pretend, of 'calling both classes
by the same name' (a nominalist excuse of purest
pedigree). What he has failed to establish is whether
there *is* an equivalence between the English and the
Japanese forms, and, if so, what exactly it consists it. In
short, he is falling back on a traditional metalanguage
to do for him the theoretical work he has shirked.

[4] E. Bach, *An Introduction to Transformational Grammars*, New York,
Holt, Rinehart and Winston, 1964, p. 176.

[5] *Ibid.*, p. 51 fn.

Applying the Western term *verb* to the Japanese forms without further ado furnishes transformational analysis with impeccable international credentials (just as an earlier generation of grammarians had applied the terminology of Latin to the description of English).

The position of philosophers with respect to the parts-of-speech doctrine was somewhat different. With historical hindsight, it is easy to see that there were only two parts of speech that Western philosophers ever needed to pay much attention to: these were 'nouns' and 'adjectives' (to give them their customary modern designations). For the rest, they could afford to restrict their interest to particular grammatical items: for example, the copula ('to be'), the negative adverb ('not'), and certain conjunctions (e.g. 'and', 'if' and 'therefore'). Verbs could be treated as combinations of copula plus adjective. This is about all the grammatical equipment required as a basis for the traditional formal logic. Even to cope with modal logic, they needed only another adverb or two (e.g. 'necessarily').

What we now call 'nouns' and 'adjectives' were special because these parts of speech had ontological implications. They supposedly pointed *beyond* language to things and properties existing in the world independently of language. (Or, at least, if they did not, then it was hard to see how human beings could ever hope to say very much at all about their environment. And in that case, *logos* itself was something of a delusion.) Thus, the argument runs, unless there actually are fish in the world, and the noun *fish* actually does 'stand for' these creatures in some way or other, then we might as well give up on pronouncements like *Fish swim*, *Fish are vertebrates*, and all similar 'fish-utterances'. Likewise, if nothing in the world is red in colour, we would do well to forego *Blood is red* and similar 'red-utterances'. Not that all nouns and adjectives are understood as standing for existing things and properties; but unless most of them were, everyday conversation would be a totally different enterprise.

In this sense, a dictionary's inventory of nouns and adjectives may be taken as giving a fair indication of what speakers of that language think their physical, social and moral world is like. For if they thought it were otherwise, then we might reasonably expect them to be using a quite different vocabulary. Either that, or they must be linguistic schizophrenics – talking about the world one way while thinking about it in another.

Perhaps, a sceptic might object, human beings are indeed schizophrenic in just this sense. And perhaps having nouns and adjectives forces us to be. Do we not talk, for instance, about a 'tall man', using two separate words where, as we know perfectly well, there is only one individual before us and his height is not separable from the rest of him? Worries of this kind have surfaced philosophically in the long debate over 'universals' and the quarrels between 'realists' and 'nominalists'. These have always been debates about the status of words and their relation to the world. But it would be a digression to go into them here. For the basic point that is relevant to the present discussion is much simpler and may be put as follows.

What is the alternative to having parts of speech which force us to divide up the world, albeit in ways which sometimes do not correspond to the physical divisions we perceive it to have? If we were not allowed a language with nouns and adjectives (for fear that these might introduce divisions in things that are indivisible), it seems we might conceivably make do with a language in which there were (i) separate words for each imaginable combination of thing and property, but (ii) no separate words for the properties as such, nor the things as such. That is to say, there would be no word for 'man' or 'tall', but only a single, unanalysable word for 'tall man'. And another for 'short man'. And another for 'man of medium height'. And so on *ad infinitum*.

But a moment's reflection should suffice to convince us that this alternative is incoherent. Collapsing nouns and adjectives into a single 'part of speech' would not take care of the problem. To avoid imposing linguistic divisions upon the indivisible, it would be necessary to proceed likewise with verbs, adverbs, and the rest. We would end up with an immense lexical inventory and a dearth of parts of speech; in short, with no viable language at all. Or, at least, none in which it was possible to make simple statements like *Fish swim* or *That man is tall*.

Strictly speaking, it might still be possible to make predications in such a language, provided it included proper names and a copula. But would there be any point in making them? It would be impossible to state anything as clear and uncomplicated as *Socrates is old*, because there would be no such isolable property as 'being old' that could be affirmed independently of umpteen other properties that might or might not apply to Socrates. Nor, by the same token, would it be possible to do anything as straightforward as calling for a pint of beer.

To realize how useless such a language would be is to take a first step towards getting to grips with the slippery notion of 'parts of speech', at least in its most primitive form. But it is no more than a start. There is still the puzzling question of what these seemingly indispensable 'parts' are parts *of*. Are they intrinsic parts of *logos* itself, or just parts of the external verbal apparatus by which *logos* is manifested in discourse? And in either case there is the no less puzzling question of what exactly determines the divisions between the parts of speech themselves.

With these issues we come to the first major crossroads that marks a professional parting of the ways between philosophers and grammarians in the ancient world. Roughly speaking, the grammarians opted for treating the parts of speech as mere word-classifications (i.e. as features of the external verbal apparatus). The philosophers, on the other hand, opted for treating the parts of speech as reflecting operations of the mind. (Thus, for example, it is significant that the philosophers began distinguishing between proper names and common nouns, whereas the grammarians continued to treat them as a single 'part'. Logically, it is important to know whether someone is referring to a unique item or to one of a kind: grammatically, it may not matter very much.)

It is here that how many parts of speech there are, and by what criteria they are distinguished, begin to emerge as important questions. But there is another matter of no less importance, which is often overlooked. In order even to raise such questions as these, it is necessary to adopt a perspective in which a language becomes detached, as it were, from its speakers. This is the point of departure for what I call 'segregational' thinking about human linguistic activity. For *onoma* and *rhema* will do well enough as the two 'parts of speech' so long as no one pays much attention to distinguishing between *what* Smith said and *the words* Smith uttered. The report 'Smith said that pigs fly' leaves the ambiguity unresolved: we are not even sure what language Smith was speaking, even though we are clear (i) that he spoke of pigs, and (ii) said that they fly. But to ask 'Did he actually say the word *pig*?' immediately moves the inquiry on to a different level altogether. And as soon as that level is reached, *onoma* and *rhema* will no longer do.

It is not difficult to appreciate that a quite different question is now being asked about the 'parts'; but less easy to grasp what that change from one level of linguistic inquiry to the other involves. And in a sense we have no viable theory of language until we can grasp that shift and explain it. An elementary requirement, one might have thought. But, sadly, no theorist in the Western tradition has so far managed to tackle it satisfactorily. Worse still, many have not even noticed the problem. Why not? Because the *fait accompli* of the shift itself successfully hides the problem and metalanguage is adopted and adapted to accommodate the shift.

How this *fait accompli* became a permanent feature of Western education is a different question again. We are dealing here, in the end, with the influence of purely contingent social factors on the course taken by the history of ideas. Once a division of intellectual labour is set up in a culture and embodied in professional practice, it becomes extraordinarily difficult to eradicate. Professions are, by definition, self-perpetuating. They claim a specific field of expertise and develop a methodology of their own. They institute a technical terminology which serves simultaneously to exclude outsiders unfamiliar with the field and to ensure that only those questions which can be couched in its terms are recognized as valid. They set up hierarchies of employment and monitor their own 'professional' qualifications. Inquiry into language is no more immune from this process than any other form of inquiry. But the irony is that in the case of language the trade-unionism involves establishing job demarcations that effectively pervert the course of inquiry; or rather, ensure that the inquiry is pursued only along lines congenial to the professions themselves.

(Anyone who doubts that this happened in the case of Western linguistic education should try to find an alternative explanation for the fact that at the present day the original Greek syllogism is still alive and well in introductory logic courses, as are 'rules' of grammar in many a school classroom; but rarely if ever are the two taught by one teacher.)

Richard Rorty makes the point that professions can outlive the paradigms that gave birth to them.[6] So they can. But they can also, in so doing, perpetuate questions which make little sense unless related to the original conditions of inquiry. The early professionalization of linguistic inquiry in Greece and Rome is highly relevant to the way in which certain problems concerning language remained on the academic slate virtually throughout the Western tradition, while others disappeared promptly and more or less permanently.

One becomes aware, for example, of a curious explanatory gap in tracing the history of the doctrine of parts of speech. The leap from asking questions about what was said to asking questions about the words uttered is a quantum leap. But it is passed over without comment because of an agreed truce between the professions involved, which tacitly stipulates that both inquiries cannot be pursued simultaneously under the same instructor.

This is not to say that the doctrine of the parts of speech escaped criticism in antiquity. Commentators were well aware that various 'authorities' differed as to

[6] R. Rorty, *Philosophy and the Mirror of Nature*, Princeton, Princeton University Press, 1979, p. 393.

how many parts of speech there were; but there is little clear-sighted discussion of the sources or implications of such disagreements. Sextus Empiricus stands virtually alone in rejecting the whole doctrine as incoherent – in which he is clearly right. He points out that if an utterance is regarded from a physical or physiological point of view as the vocal production of sounds, then although it has 'parts' they are not parts of speech in the sense in which speech is something comprehended and comprehensible. On the other hand, if it is regarded from a semantic point of view (i.e. as meaningful) it is unclear in what sense its incorporeal 'meaning' has any parts at all.[7] He might have added a third criticism: if it is held that what identifies the separate 'parts' are *correlations* between sound and meaning, then these do not in any case correspond in any systematic way to the units recognized by the doctrine.

What Sextus Empiricus is commenting on is, in effect, the highly unsatisfactory product of the division of labour between grammarians and logicians. As a result of this division – to put it in the least misleading modern metalinguistic terms available – the sentence became the province of one profession while the proposition became the province of the other. But at the very moment when the legitimacy of this separation was recognized, something happened to the object of inquiry. Speech, the thing that had originally had 'parts', was replaced by two other objects, each of which might also be claimed to have 'parts', but in a different sense. It was no longer speech that was under analysis but two separate reductions derived from speech. That substitution was the intellectual price paid for institutionalizing the division of labour in the first place.

---

[7] *Adversus Mathematicos* I, 155ff.

This professional partition fudged a number of important issues and allowed some to slip down the crack in between. Speech was henceforth treated as yielding a product that could be analysed without reference to the producer or the occasion of production. To analyse *Socrates is bald* – either grammatically or logically – we do not need to know who said it, when, to whom, or why. This was the turning point which set Western metalinguistics off on the segregational track it still follows at the present day. The notion that the product has an internal structure *of its own* which in the end depends neither on the producer nor on the production process is the segregational assumption that became the key to analysing all verbal manifestations of *logos*.

Once this happens, speech is no longer the whole it once was. For it cannot be re-synthesized from the set of units introduced under the new regime which divides sentence from proposition. By analytic fission, the original *onoma* splits into the logician's subject and the grammarian's noun or noun phrase, while the *rhema* dissolves into the logician's predicate and the grammarian's verb or verb phrase. The speaker and the listener, who between them originally held speech together as a coherent human activity, drop out of the picture altogether. The case is then as desperate as Humpty Dumpty's. All the king's horses and all the king's men will never be able to put speech together again.

Chapter 3
ONE-DIMENSIONAL SPEECH

The course the ancient grammarians opted for was a simple one. They chose to concentrate on those features of the speech process that were audible and visible (roughly, the sounds and the movements of the articulatory organs). The rest – everything that was neither audible nor visible – they relegated to a position of secondary importance, or else did not bother with at all. In short, they focussed on what was immediately (and publicly) available to sense perception. In this respect, grammar is the first form of empiricism in Western 'philosophy of language'.

Why the grammarians chose this as their province I will leave on one side for the moment, in order to bring out the consequences of that choice. It meant that anything that started out as a human utterance ended up, as far as the grammarians were concerned, as the utterance *of* a certain sequence of units. Any features of the original utterance that resisted the compression were discarded. They simply did not 'belong'. Occam's razor was a relatively late (and relatively benign) version of a professional instrument that grammarians had wielded ruthlessly for centuries.

This solution has remained in vogue in grammatical circles from the school of ancient Alexandria down to the structuralists of Geneva and the generativists of Cambridge, Mass. Its effect is that 'linearity' (so-called) automatically becomes a defining property of the

35

linguistic sign. For it is a strategy that requires the selection of a single dimension along which to exhibit, compare and locate the various *perceptible* features of utterances. And the obvious dimension to select is time. (This was never made explicit by the grammarians of antiquity, but is overtly recognized by their twentieth-century successors, and even proclaimed as one of the foundational principles of linguistic analysis.[1])

The above caveat concerning 'so-called' linearity is appropriate here, because the term *linearity*, although constantly used nowadays, is a misnomer. The linguistic sign does not have the characteristics of a visible line (which would make it two-dimensional at least). What the term *linearity* is intended to imply is that all the parts occur in unique temporal succession. The human voice (it is claimed) cannot – unlike certain musical instruments – produce two sounds simultaneously; which, translated into the phonetics of speech, means that human beings cannot say more than one thing at a time.

Insofar as this is a claim about the impossibility of any single individual saying simultaneously [t] and [d] or *John loves Mary* and *Mary loves John*, it is unexceptionable. If we want to say both, then we have to choose to say one first and the other subsequently. The human vocal apparatus is not constructed in such a way as to allow the speaker to utter both at once. (On Mars, perhaps the inhabitants may be able to manage it, but that would require the Martian vocal tract to have more cavities and articulators than ours. But if it has, then the consequences are doubtless profound for the Martian language or languages, about which little is known at present.)

---

[1] F. de Saussure, *Course in General Linguistics*, trans. R. Harris, London, Duckworth, 1983, pp. 69–70.

Where the one-thing-at-a-time claim becomes more dubious is when theorists transfer it from being a claim about the phonetics of the terrestrial vocal tract to a claim about the structure of the sentence (or its parts). But this conflation is the (intended) outcome of opting for a one-dimensional view of speech in the first place. In other words, it is unsurprising that we find ourselves obliged to concede that we cannot utter two sentences at once, because the grammarian has defined *sentence* for us in such a way that any two things that could be uttered 'at once' would never qualify as sentences. (Thus even if I deliberately choose what I say – as politicians commonly do – so that one section of my audience will take me to be saying one thing, while another section of my audience will take me to be saying something different, those two things could never, in the grammarian's tally, add up to uttering more than one sentence at a time.) The same goes for phrases, words, consonants and vowels – all the crucial units.

The grammatical doctrine of ambiguity (lexical or syntactic) acquires its rationale here. Recognizing ambiguities – but treating them as 'accidental' imperfections of language – is a strategy for preserving intact the more basic assumption about the 'linearity' of speech. Thus saying *I could give her a ring* still counts as uttering one sentence and not two simultaneously, even though it might be quite unclear – and even intended to be unclear – whether what I have in mind is making a telephone call or marrying her.

Why this one-dimensional restriction? Because it gives the grammarian the advantage of being able to treat analysis as *segmentation*. In short, the foundation of grammar in the Western tradition is a procedure by which a consecutive string of vocalization is segmented into non-overlapping constituent parts.

The ancient grammarians, furthermore, had ready to hand a technology which enabled them to systematize this segmental analysis of speech in a clear and simple – if somewhat rough-and-ready – way. The technology in question was alphabetic writing. The form of segmentation they adopted as basic is perfectly familiar nowadays to the Western schoolchild. The reason for this is that the writing system has remained more or less unchanged. Thus we find it unremarkable to write *cat* as a sequence of three separate symbols, even though the word as uttered is a single continuous stream of sound with no internal breaks.

The extent to which familiarity with particular writing practices has influenced views of how language works is a topic which deserves more detailed treatment than it can be given here. But the initial point to be made is that in the Western tradition the grammarian's essential business, as the etymology of the term *grammarian* itself indicates, was originally with writing and induction into literacy. (Cf. Gk. *grammata*, 'letters [sc. of the alphabet]'; *grammatistes*, 'one who teaches the *grammata*; a schoolmaster'.) And *for that purpose* it is very useful to adopt a 'one-dimensional' view of the basic linguistic units. For then it becomes possible (i) to count them, and (ii) to state exhaustively the rules of ('linear') concatenation for forming larger units, which, in turn, can then (iii) be counted and treated as exhaustively analysable into sequences of discrete smaller units, and (iv) most importantly of all, to establish a set of agreed correlations between speech and writing. Acquaintance with those correlations then becomes an educational achievement in its own right (i.e. 'knowing how to spell') and can be treated as the foundation of literacy.

As a historical footnote, it is perhaps worth adding that by formalizing this reduction, Western grammarians were in fact treading the path long established by Western poets. They were carrying over into a literate culture the analytic techniques of pre-literate poetry. Greek grammar is inconceivable without Homer. Homeric metre is meaningless for any who are not *meropes brotoi*. Dividing and counting go together. But it is interesting that when Western metres abandoned syllable length in favour of stress as their 'counting' criterion, grammar was already so professionalized that it could resist any pressure to change its own rationale of reduction.

Given the one-dimensional compression, every utterance can then be treated by the grammarian as the product of rendering words audible. (This is exactly what we find in the earliest known definition of grammar – by Dionysius Thrax – which includes 'reading aloud'. This was obviously an extremely important practical accomplishment for the student.) In this manner, a curious inversion occurs in construing the relationship between speech and writing. The latter comes to provide the model for interpreting the former.

This way of developing a basic metalinguistics makes it possible to treat speaking as 'pronouncing aloud the sentence(s) one has already formulated in one's head'. So what began as a matter of pedagogical expediency ends up promoting a certain view of the psychology of speech; and this view in turn has considerable implications for linguistic theory.

The logician, on the other hand, had no motivation whatsoever for pursuing anything like the grammarian's programme. On the contrary, as will become evident below, in certain respects the logician could not *afford* to compress speech into these one-dimensional concatenations; for that would actually have made a comprehensive treatment of patterns like the syllogism impossible. That is to say, if

All men are mortal
Socrates is a man
Socrates is mortal

is regarded merely as a trio of *sentences*, then there is no generalization to be derived therefrom that would be of interest to the logician. From the grammarian's point of view, each sentence is an autonomous, self-contained unit. The three could occur in any order without affecting their identity. For the logician's purposes (as also, it might be added, for the rhetorician's), there has to be something more involved – at the very least a 'train of thought' that carries over from one of these sentences *in sequence* to the next and unites the three into a single piece of reasoning.

So the professional parting of the ways between the type of linguistic inquiry pursued by the grammarian and that pursued by the logician is not the result of mere chance, but relates to certain intellectual and pedagogic objectives within a specific educational system. In effect, both professions say: 'Let us treat speech *as if* such-and-such were the case': but the 'such-and-such' in the two instances is different and both involve an oversimplification.

One conspicuous feature of this oversimplification in the grammarian's domain is that the intonational features of the utterance – extremely important in actual conversation, not to mention public speaking – are virtually ignored. Not only is it impossible to accommodate them as 'parts of speech', but any attempt to accommodate them *at all* risks disturbing the convenient fiction of linearity. The awkwardness survives in modern linguistics, where desperate attempts have been made to fit intonation into a theory of phonemes. In spite of this, the apologetic and tell-tale term *suprasegmental* survives as witness to a long-standing reluctance to treat this dimension of speech as anything other than an addition 'on top of' (*supra-*) a more fundamental linear sequence. (Thus the contrast between *You saw him* and *You saw him?*, which is indicated graphically – insofar as it is indicated at all – by the addition of a single character (= ?) at the end of a sequence of characters, corresponds to a whole series of phonetic differences which are treated as 'suprasegmental' features of the utterances in question.)

This aspect of speech does not get even a passing nod of recognition from the logician. (What would the intonation of a proposition sound like? A proposition is not, after all, a mantra, even though it has attracted exaggerated respect from mystically inclined Western philosophers.) But, obvious though the point may be, making it all the same serves to underscore the extent to which, after the professional separation between rhetoric, logic and grammar, we are dealing with the manipulation of reductions which are at one remove from speech, and not with any comprehensive investigation of speech itself as a human activity.

This may be the place at which to consider a justification often advanced for the institutionalized separation of different kinds of linguistic study. It runs as follows. Speech is an extremely complex business; far too complex to be dealt with from any single academic perspective. Consequently, it is not merely inevitable but essential that different disciplines should divide it up between them if any progress at all is to be made in its investigation. Thus while it is true that the rhetorician, the logician, the grammarian, the phonetician, the lexicographer, the conversation analyst, the speech therapist, etc. pay attention only to limited aspects of the subject, and ignore those which do not fall within their chosen province, this is actually the best way of proceeding. Otherwise, we should have simply a muddle.

The short answer to that is that we have a muddle anyway. The apologia would be more convincing if the lauded strategy of specialized studies were in fact the product of a concerted academic policy for the systematic and comprehensive investigation of human speech. But that is far from being the case. No one sat down and first asked 'How can speech best be studied?'. The academic patchwork we are confronted with today is purely negative in character: it is the result of the *lack* of interest by particular disciplines and sub-disciplines in anything which does not cross the narrow path of their tunnel vision. Nowhere is this more obvious than when we consider the inventory of what is subsumed under the rubric 'philosophy of language'. If one asks, for example, why philosophy of language does not include any discussion of, say, phonology or bilingualism, the answer is not 'Because those subjects do not *need* any philosophical commentary', but 'Because those subjects are not seen by philosophers as having any relevance to traditional philosophical concerns.' The disciplines operate like government departments, declining all responsibility for anything it is not to their own advantage to claim.

*   *   *

Now let us pass on to considering in detail this controversial one-dimensional monstrosity, the sentence. The traditional story told by Western grammarians went

something like this. A sentence is a 'complete' concatenation of linearly discrete elements, each of which can
be assigned to a determinate 'part of speech', and each
of which can be subdivided into its constituent vowels
and consonants. Thus *Fish swim* is composed of noun
+ verb. *Fish swim slowly* is composed of noun + verb
+ adverb. *Little fish swim slowly* is composed of
adjective + noun + verb + adverb. And so on.

Why does the concatenation take place in that order?
Well, presumably the concatenation has to take place in
some order or other. Granted; but why would not *any*
order do? Because, according to the grammarian's story,
there is an overarching relationship between (i) the
atomic phonetic units, (ii) the parts of speech and (iii)
the sentence structure. This relationship ensures, for
instance, that *Big fish swim slowly* has the same
grammatical analysis as *Little fish swim slowly*. For *big*
and *little* are both adjectives. Hence the only difference
between the two sentences reduces to the phonetic and
semantic differences between the individual words *big*
and *little*. These would be further reduced if *big* and
little were synonymous. Then saying 'Big fish swim
slowly' would be exactly the same thing as saying 'Little
fish swim slowly' *except for* the phonetic differences
between *big* and *little*. Or, to put it another way, substituting *big* for *little* in the linear concatenation is the
(unique) operation which changes *Little fish swim
slowly* into *Big fish swim slowly*.

This trivial example encapsulates centuries of Western
metalinguistics. But it also reveals the Achilles' heel of
the Western grammarian. The strategy adopted enables
the grammarian to exhibit and analyse any given
utterance as a concatenation of units which can be
correlated plausibly with perceptible phases in the
speech act, as the underlying metalinguistic strategy

requires. Nevertheless, it is far from obvious how the 'parts of speech' themselves, which mediate between the atomic units and a maximum concatenation (= sentence), can themselves be defined in such terms. The way the ancient grammarians solved this problem was to appeal to the non-perceptible (i.e. inaudible and invisible) sections of the speech process. This, in short, is where 'meanings' come into the professional act of the grammarian.

When we look at the definitions of the eight parts of speech supplied by Dionysius Thrax we find that only two of them are defined purely in terms of linear concatenation (relative to others). These correspond to what are nowadays called the *preposition* (Gk. *prothesis*) and the *article* (Gk. *arthron*). All the other definitions appeal in some way or other to what the words falling into that class are supposed to 'mean'.

Thus, for example, Dionysius's definition of *onoma* tells us that the *onoma* designates a body or thing: illustrative examples given are the Greek words for 'stone', 'education', 'man', 'horse' and 'Socrates'.[2] Now it is clear that we cannot simply by listening to any of these words when uttered, or by watching the movements of the tongue, lips, etc., determine whether it designates a body or thing, much less a stone, education, man, horse, etc. What the word is intended or understood to designate (by the speaker or the hearer) depends on processes going on in other parts of the speech programme, parts which are not open to direct examination by audition or inspection; or else on actions (such as gesture) which lie outside the programme altogether.

---

[2]   J. Lallot, *La Grammaire de Denys le Thrace*, Paris, CNRS, 1989, p. 49.

Consequently the grammarian's agenda for surveying the 'external' manifestations of *logos* cannot, it seems, be carried out in a self-contained or independent manner. It must rely at least to some extent on the grammarian's assumptions about the 'internal' workings of *logos*, i.e. on correlations between sounds and meanings. It was not until much later in the Western tradition – not in fact until the twentieth century – that linguists addressed the question of whether it might be possible to supply a complete structural analysis of the sentence in terms of purely external (formal) criteria, i.e. without relying at all on assumptions about the meanings of its parts. (The eventual result of this was 'distributional' analysis.[3]) But the Greeks never considered the possibility seriously. For them, that would have been tantamount to puzzling over a quite useless question; namely, whether it was possible to learn to speak a language without having any idea of what one was saying in it. Not merely a useless question, but a perverse and even nonsensical one, inasmuch as speech without *logos* was for them a contradiction in terms.

This brings us at last to the question of the rationale underlying the metalinguistic programme of the ancient grammarians; and the answer lies in their professional function as language-teachers. This set them apart both from the logicians and from the rhetoricians. A language-teacher is required, by definition, to reduce languages – as far as possible – to what is explicitly and systematically teachable from scratch. Now there are cultures which have neither language-teachers nor language-teaching in this sense. And this is doubtless

---

[3] Cf. Z. S. Harris, 'Distributional structure', *Word*, vol. 10, no. 2/3, 1954, pp. 146–62.

why they typically lack the kind of terminology that European education takes for granted (even though they may have a highly developed metalanguage reflecting other concerns). It is only when language-teaching becomes part of a formal course of instruction that anything like the basic concerns of the grammarians of Greece and Rome begins to make sense at all, and 'parts' have to be postulated in order to formulate 'rules'.

Now it is possible to learn a language without undergoing any formal instruction whatever. Just as it is possible to learn to do many things (usually by imitating those who can already do such things, by joining in, by trial and error). But as soon as there is any question of explicit instruction – whether it be in how to speak a language, how to bake a cake, or how to mend a puncture – what is needed is a terminology which corresponds to the units and operations of that instruction. It must be a terminology which allows questions about the instruction to be asked, answers to be given by the instructor, and pedagogically useful generalizations to be made. The grammarian's metalanguage developed in the Western tradition corresponded exactly to those requirements – *and to no more.* That was why the grammarian's one-dimensional 'sentence' was never a very useful unit for the logician from the start.

Chapter 4
LOGICAL LOOPHOLES

The logicians of Graeco-Roman antiquity, like the grammarians, were teachers. But their aims and their point of departure were different. In the first place, they were not interested in language-teaching as such. Their students were already assumed to be perfectly competent in the language(s) in question. The domain of logic was taken to comprise the processes of reasoning. The term *logic* itself suggests that these are the essence or foundation of *logos*.

Logicians were from the beginning ranked 'above' grammarians in the hierarchy of educational progress. A similar hierarchical assumption has remained in place down to the present day. Being able to speak a language fluently is still regarded as no guarantee of any ability to employ that language for the formulation of cogent arguments, or the detection and exposure of flaws in the arguments presented by others.

Nevertheless speech remained, for the logicians, a prerequisite for reasoning, since animals did not have it. However eloquently a dog may bark it cannot, as a philosopher once observed, tell you that its parents were poor but honest. *A fortiori*, a dog cannot reason. It cannot draw any inferences about its parents. Reasoning, in this perspective, is a matter of proceeding from a starting point to a conclusion by steps which (i) can be specified, and (ii) do not slip inadvertently from truth into falsehood.

47

To conceive of logic thus is to conceive of it as a kind of verbal arithmetic. An incorrect inference is regarded as analogous to an error of addition or subtraction. This ancient conception was to prevail throughout the Western tradition as the anchor of all philosophical discussion. Although it was not until many centuries later that any philosopher attempted to demonstrate explicitly the continuity between the basic concepts of arithmetic and those of logic, this continuity had always been taken informally for granted. Hobbes, for instance, writes:

> When a man *Reasoneth*, hee does nothing else but conceive a summe totall, from *Addition* of parcels; or conceive a Remainder, from *Substraction* of one summe from another: which (if it be done by Words,) is conceiving of the consequence of the names of all the parts, to the name of the whole; or from the names of the whole and one part, to the name of the other part.[1]

It remained for later logicians to embark on formalizing this conception of logic as verbal arithmetic. Boole, author of *Laws of Thought* (1854) has been described as 'the first to perfect in quasi-mathematical form a statement of the principles of logic'.[2] The *Principia Mathematica* (1910) of Russell and Whitehead is often regarded as the culmination of this endeavour. Given the connection between dividing and counting, all this can be viewed as yet a further development of the ancient concept of human beings as *meropes brotoi*.

---

[1] *Leviathan*, I, 5.

[2] R. M. Eaton, *General Logic*, London, Scribner, 1931, p. 360.

The crucial point in this Western development of the arithmetical model of thinking and its metalanguage is reached when it is realized that all depends on the units taken as basic to operations of reasoning (= calculating). Very early in the European tradition it was recognized that there is a problem about taking those units to be words or combinations of words (in the sense in which the grammarian deals with words). The author of the ancient text known as the *Dissoi Logoi* points out that the words 'I am an initiate' may be uttered both by an initiate and by one who is not.[3] If this is accepted, it seems that we have to conclude either that one and the same form of words may be both true and false, or else that what is true or false is not the form of words itself. If the former is the case, it frustrates any enterprise of formulating the principles of valid inference on the basis of relations between sentences. If the latter is the case, then the metalinguistic terms 'true' and 'false' cannot properly apply to sentences at all, but must be deemed to apply to something else. Western logic chose the latter option, and thereby conjured into existence what was later called the 'proposition'. This gave rise to endless debate about the status of the proposition, the relationship between propositions and sentences, how to derive the proposition from the meanings of the words used, etc. The debate has continued down to the present century.

What is involved here is the introduction of a new metalinguistic unit (i.e. the 'proposition') in order to bypass the problems encountered if the actual words uttered are treated as the basis of logic. The grammarians of antiquity, unlike the logicians, did not

---

[3] W. Kneale and M. Kneale, *The Development of Logic*, rev. ed., Oxford, Clarendon, 1984, p. 16.

need to adopt this new unit, because it answered to no requirement in their own professional programme. Nor did the logicians themselves immediately reach a consensus about how the new unit should be defined or what it should be called.

In part this was because philosophers could not decide exactly where truth and falsity lay. Plato hops uncomfortably from one foot to the other on the issue. In the *Theaetetus* knowledge is identified with true opinion. But what is opinion? Is it a psychological phenomenon? Socrates defines thinking, in a famous reply, as 'the talk which the soul holds with itself', and forming an opinion as coming to a decision when talking to oneself in silence. Thus it is possible, as modern commentators have observed, to

> detect at least two possible answers to our question in Plato. Sometimes it is suggested that the proper subject of the predicates 'true' and 'false' is a sentence or verbal pattern. At other times it is suggested that the proper subject is a psychological event which occurs when the verbal pattern is formed or used by a person in overt or silent discourse.[4]

Aristotle, who – unlike Plato – was interested in formalizing logic, could hardly rest content with this non-solution. But although modern translators often present him to us as distinguishing between 'sentences' and 'propositions', this is arguably anachronistic. From a modern point of view it is not quite as simple as treating one set of items (propositions) as a subset of the other (sentences); whereas that is exactly how Aristotle seems to treat the relationship. What Aristotle says (*De Interpretatione* 17a) is that not every *logos* (? =

----

[4] *Ibid.*, p. 18.

'sentence') is an *apophansis* (? = 'proposition'). But he illustrates the difference by pointing out that whereas a prayer is a *logos*, it is not an *apophansis*, because 'it neither has truth nor has falsity', and therefore its study falls into the domain of rhetoric or poetry.

This certainly suggests that all Aristotle is saying here is simply (i) that not every meaningful utterance is an assertion, (ii) that only assertions are true or false, and (iii) these alone are the utterances the logician is interested in. There is no hint at all, in short, that Aristotle is trying to distinguish between, for example, the *sentence* 'Man is an animal' and the *proposition* 'Man is an animal'. What *is* clear, however, is that he is trying to restrict logic to basic units of which one can sensibly say 'This is true', 'This is false', 'Suppose this were true...', 'Suppose this were false...', 'If this were true...', 'If this were false...', and so on.

But it is by no means impossible to imagine a school of philosophy choosing the option which the Western tradition rejected; that is to say, developing a 'logic' based strictly on relations between sentences. Something like this seems to have been attempted by the *Ming chia* school in China. Its best known example is provided by the celebrated 'paradox of the white horse', which to a Western way of thinking is not so much a paradox as a plain absurdity. But it is interesting to ask why. The traditional Chinese story tells how Kung-sun Lung, passing a frontier on his horse, was stopped by guards who told him that horses were not allowed to pass.

Kung-sun Lung replied: "My horse is white, and a white horse is not a horse." And so saying, he passed with his horse.[5]

[5] Fung Yu-Lan, *A Short History of Chinese Philosophy*, ed. D. Bodde, New York, Free Press, 1948, p. 87.

That we find it hard to follow the (implied) argument should itself serve as a reminder of the extent to which assumptions concerning words and reasoning are culture-bound. That is to say, our (Western) problem with making sense of Kung-sun Lung's answer to the frontier guards, and the guards' apparent acquiescence, has to do with our readiness to follow the path of Aristotle and his successors. That path already assumes that logic can be – and must be – divorced from 'mere' words. It requires – *in us* – an imaginative leap to be able to 'think ourselves into' a position where what Kung-sun Lung says is *automatically* convincing. In other words, we experience a dissociation or lack of fit between (i) the (translated) verbal report of what the sage said and (ii) the conclusion in (apparently) logical terms, i.e. that Kung-sun Lung on his horse was *not* contravening the prohibition on horses passing the frontier.

In order to understand the example aright, we have to set aside some possible misconceptions of what is at issue. For instance, it is *not* like arguing that a ban on importing books does not apply to newspapers because 'a newspaper is not a book'. Nor is it like arguing that a ban on importing drugs does not apply to tea because 'tea is not a drug'. These are problems any Western lawyer can cope with. But Western lawyers cannot deal with the contention that a white horse is not a horse. Any such contention would be laughed out of court (and the guilty barrister hooted out of chambers).

Some have traced the root of the problem to the grammatical fact that the Chinese language has no definite or indefinite article. Fung argues that

in Chinese, such terms as "horse," "the horse," and "a horse" are all designated by the one word *ma* or "horse". It would seem, therefore, that fundamentally the word *ma* denotes the universal concept, "horse"...'[6]

This explanation supposedly fits in with the three arguments given in the *Kung-sun Lung-tzu* in support of the claim that a white horse is not a horse. 1. The word 'horse' denotes a shape, while the word 'white' denotes a colour. Denoting a shape is not the same as denoting a colour. Therefore 'white horse' and 'horse' are not the same. 2. When a horse is required, a black horse or a yellow horse will do. But not when a white horse is required. Therefore 'white horse' and 'horse' are not the same. 3. Imagine a colourless horse. That would be different from a white horse. Therefore 'white horse' and 'horse' are not the same.[7]

The first two arguments, according to Fung, can be 'translated' into Western terms as an argument from intension and an argument from extension respectively, while the third simply insists on the difference between the two universals 'horseness' and 'white-horseness'. The point to note here is that it would be a mistake to try to fit all this into the canonical pattern of the Aristotelian syllogism. In other words, the argument is not:

All horses are colourless
This animal is white
Therefore, it is not a horse.

On the contrary, that would not only attribute gratuitously to the sage a major premiss he does not need, but also conflict with the data of the anecdote, in which

---

[6] *Ibid.*, p. 90.
[7] *Ibid.*, pp. 87–8.

Kung-sun Lung apparently concedes that he is riding a horse ('My horse is white.'). That is the feature which makes the whole business puzzling to Western eyes; but it is also what renders the example instructive if we are interested in clarifying the presuppositions of the Western syllogism. That is to say, the lack of fit between the syllogistic pattern and Kung-sun Lung's reasoning hinges on the fact that the Western syllogism needs to have an existential generalization as its major premiss.

This is why students are taught to recast statements into 'logical form' (as it is sometimes called). Thus, for instance, *It will probably rain when the barometer is low* becomes in the logician's classroom *All occasions on which the barometer is low are occasions on which rain is probable.* Similarly, *Few philosophers are wealthy* becomes *The class of wealthy philosophers is a small class.*[8] These 'recastings' give the logician's game away in a manner which is quite revealing and highly relevant to the present discussion. For, patently, what is presupposed is that the original sentence and its recast form are synonymous or 'express the same proposition'. But where does this guarantee come from? Its validity cannot be demonstrated by syllogistic reasoning itself, for the whole problem turns on the fact that certain sentences are not 'suited' to the syllogistic pattern.

Traditionally, the four basic sentence-types admitted as acceptable for syllogistic treatment were the 'universal affirmative' (*All men are mortal*), the 'universal negative' (*No men are mortal*), the 'particular affirmative' (*Some men are mortal. Socrates is mortal*) and the 'particular negative' (*Some men are not mortal. Socrates is not mortal*).[9] Thus, as one logician observes, the traditional

---

[8] These examples are from W. A. Sinclair, *The Traditional Formal Logic*, London, Methuen, 1937.

logic 'insists upon a high degree of conventionalized simplification in restating the complex expressions of ordinary speech in order to express them in one or other of the four recognized forms'.[10]

This 'simplification' (= reduction) of the forms of ordinary speech, so essential to the logician's enterprise, is a metalinguistic manipulation which deserves careful study in its own right. For it tells us a great deal about the metalinguistic framework which Western logic implicitly takes for granted. Here we see where and why the logician *does* need the sentence and, more generally, how it is that Western logic needs grammar. The differences between the logician's various 'logical forms' have to be defined, at least in the first instance, in the metalanguage of grammar. That is to say, *affirmative, negative, universal,* and the rest have to be spelled out in terms of particular constructions and the use of particular grammatical devices (such as the word *not*). Unless this metalinguistic endeavour were viable, the logician's programme would never get off the ground. Generalization (of the kind the syllogism requires) would be impossible and every argument would have to be treated as a one-off case.

To return to Kung-sun Lung's reasoning, however, we shall never understand it if we take him to be proceeding in the manner of the typical Western logician, i.e. trying to reach a 'particular negative' conclusion (*This animal is not a horse*) on the basis of a 'universal affirmative' major premiss plus a 'particular affirmative' minor.

---

[9] *Socrates is mortal* can be treated as a kind of minimum case of *Some men are mortal* (= *At least one man is mortal*). And likewise *mutatis mutandis* for *Socrates is not mortal*.

[10] Sinclair, *op. cit.*, p. 28.

That may be obvious enough. But the next point is less so. Although Fung's exegesis of the paradox, summarized above, is perceptive, the absence of an indefinite article in Chinese is something of a red herring. In other words, even if there were an indefinite article in Chinese, there would still be a problem, and it has nothing to do with Chinese grammar. It turns on the fact that the guards try to stop the sage *because*, patently, they think they detect a violation of the ban on horses. If we go for the 'grammatical' explanation of what happened next, we have to suppose that what the sage says convinces the guards that they have misunderstood the ban. But this does not make much sense either. In other words, if the sage's point is merely one about the relationship between the universals 'horseness' and 'whiteness', more astute guards at the frontier would have agreed with him, but nevertheless insisted that the sage was welcome to take the colour with him, provided the horse remained behind.

There is a simpler explanation, which makes no appeal to universals at all. This involves seeing that the puzzle could equally well be set up in a language which *did* have the grammatical equipment of articles, and therefore could perfectly well express the difference between 'horse(ness)' and 'a horse'. All that is required to set it up is the assumption that logic operates with words as its basic units. From this it follows immediately and self-evidently that a ban on horses is not a ban on white horses. Only a ban on white horses is a ban on white horses. The guards have invoked the wrong ban. A Western lawyer would immediately feel more comfortable with the case, viewed in these terms. In other words, it would be like defending someone who had been prosecuted on the wrong charge. There is no need for any rigmarole about universals and colourless horses. Quite simply, whoever formulated the ban had not formulated it carefully enough. This is a form of defence very familiar in Western courts, and it does not involve any 'inscrutable' Oriental reasoning at all.

What it does involve, however, is a different metalinguistic perspective. In this perspective, to put it in the simplest terms possible, words 'say what they say, but no more'. The basic Western assumption, on the contrary, is that there is always something more than what words say, and this 'something more' reaches beyond words to independently given objects. This is the assumption on which Western logic is founded, and it is what underlies the Western difficulty in interpreting 'a white horse is not a horse' as anything other than a universal negative (= 'no white horse is a horse') which is self-evidently false.

The alternative, which we glimpse in the 'white horse paradox', involves limiting logic strictly to what is said. Only then does it become possible to argue, as in effect the *Kung-sun Lung-tzu* does, that *because* the predicate 'white' and the predicate 'horse' are different predicates, any referent picked out by combining the two predicates is not the same as what is picked out by either predicate by itself. Class inclusion is from this point of view simply an irrelevance: it relates to the structure of the world, not to the structure of language. Thus 'a white horse is not a horse' is not a self-contradiction because it is not an empirical generalization (and hence does not have to be taken as denying that white horses belong to the class of horses). It states a metalinguistic principle, *viz.* that the two non-identical predicates 'horse' and 'white' do not identify the same referent(s). Thus even if there is one and only one animal in question, to speak of 'this horse' and 'this white horse' is immediately to speak of two different things. From this perspective, a ban on horses *tout court* is hopelessly vague. It is patently *not* a ban on all horses. But nor does it state which kinds of horses it applies to. It is this logical loophole that Kung-sun Lung rides through on his white horse.

In order to see this as a logical loophole in the first place, we have to see the relationship between language and the world in what is, for Western eyes, a reversed perspective. As long as we fail to adopt this perspective, the argument *still* does not make sense; i.e. from the difference between the predicates 'horse' and 'white', it simply does not follow (by Western reasoning) that a white horse is not a horse. Why is this? Because the typical Western assumption is that language is or should be a reflection of the world. If there is only one horse out there and it is white, then that immediately settles the matter, i.e. falsifies any claim that a white horse is not a horse. But do we have to look at language that way? Instead of supposing that language is or should be a reflection of the world, why should we not suppose that the world is or should be a reflection of language? Then it will be words that determine whether things are 'the same' or 'not the same'. And there will be no question of devising terminologies to match already given sets of items; but, on the contrary, a serious question as to whether items that do exist conform to already established designations.

Exactly this perspective lies at the basis of the Confucian doctrine of *cheng ming* (or 'the rectification of names'). According to this doctrine, the world is in the best possible state when its condition conforms exactly to the designations provided by language, and in a worse state when it fails to do so, for whatever reason. The remedy is to bring the state of the world back into line with language.

When Duke Ching of Ch'i inquired of Confucius the principles of government, Confucius answered saying: 'Let the ruler be ruler, the minister minister; let the father be father, and the son son.' 'Excellent!' said the Duke. 'For truly if the ruler be not ruler, the minister not minister, if the father be not father, and the son not son, though grain exist, shall I be allowed to eat it?'[11]

As in the case of 'a white horse is not a horse', the advice 'let the ruler be ruler' has to be interpreted on the basis of the right metalinguistic assumptions if we are to make any sense of it. Both dicta sound absurd when translated into English (or any other European language) not because of any grammatical differences between the languages, but because the translation does not allow for a basic difference in metalinguistic perspective. The privileged direction of interpretation in the West is from words to things, not vice versa. This is why 'a white horse is not a horse' is automatically interpreted by Westerners as an existential generalization. And 'let the ruler be ruler' sounds silly for a related reason, i.e. because a ruler in fact already rules. (How else would he be a ruler?).

It is the Duke's reply to Confucius which reveals the depth of the gulf separating the Western from the Confucian perspective. What use is grain if you cannot eat it? Again, the relevance of the remark is perhaps not immediately apparent to the Western reader. Grain is a natural product, but it is cultivated by human beings for a human purpose. If there were grain but one could not eat it, the times would be out of joint. It might still be *called* 'grain', but abusively so, since the word would

---

[11] Fung Yu-Lan, *A History of Chinese Philosophy*, trans. D. Bodde, 2nd ed., vol. 1, Princeton, Princeton University Press, 1952, p. 60.

now be divorced from the human cycle that gave it its meaning. Likewise, if the state of society is such that its members are no longer fulfilling the roles and duties implicit in the designations *ruler, minister, father* and *son*, then society has come to a sorry pass. The social order has broken down. But that order – the order in terms of which one makes the judgment that something is amiss – does not come from society itself but from the categories and relationships implicit in the language by which society is described. As in the case of the white horse, it is language which gives us the norms by which to judge reality.

Words, on this view, do not have meanings which are at the mercy of adventitious changes in human behaviour or upheavals in the ways of the world. They are in some sense established independently of the world and its history and independently too of the collectivity of language-users. The Confucian theory might perhaps be described as a theory of Platonic Forms, but one in which the Forms, far from lurking in some remote and otherworldly realm, are ever-present in language.

However, rather than compare Confucius with Plato, it is perhaps more instructive in the first instance to contrast Confucius's position with the more down-to-earth Western approach to the relation between language and society that we find in Thucydides. In Book 3 of his *History of the Peloponnesian War*, Thucydides offers the following comment on the aftermath of the civil war in Corcyra.

So revolutions broke out in city after city, and in places where the revolutions occurred late the knowledge of what had happened previously in other places caused still new extravagances of revolutionary zeal, expressed by an elaboration in the methods of seizing

power and by unheard of atrocities in revenge. To fit
in with the change of events, words, too, had to
change their usual meanings. What used to be
described as a thoughtless act of aggression was now
regarded as the courage one would expect to find in a
party member; to think of the future and wait was
merely another way of saying one was a coward; any
idea of moderation was just an attempt to disguise
one's unmanly character; ability to understand a
question from all sides meant that one was totally
unfitted for action. Fanatical enthusiasm was the
mark of a real man, and to plot against an enemy
behind his back was perfectly legitimate self-defence.[12]

Thucydides blames these revolutions for 'a general
deterioration of character throughout the Greek world'.
Now Confucius would doubtless agree that the kind of
breakdown in social order described by Thucydides is
deplorable. But whereas, according to Thucydides,
what happened was that words changed their meanings
to match new standards of behaviour, a Confucian
analysis would claim, on the contrary, that the new
standards of behaviour failed to conform to the
(unchanging) meaning of the words used to describe
human actions. The reason why Thucydides' analysis
would be unacceptable from a Confucian point of view
is important. If language changes in conformity with
human behaviour, then the doctrine of the rectification
of names becomes vacuous. For whatever people, at a
given time and place, decide to call 'honourable' then *is*
honourable, whatever they call 'good' *is* good; and so
on. Thus language no longer provides the norms by

---

[12] *History of the Peloponnesian War*, trans. R. Warner, rev. ed., London,
Penguin, 1972, p. 242.

which to judge reality. We slide into what is, at best, a facile relativism, and at worst – for Confucius, at least – linguistic and social anarchy.

*   *   *

If Confucius and Kung-sun Lung had not existed, it might have been necessary to invent them; at least, for purposes of illustrating the point that the use of metalinguistic predicates like 'true' and 'false' (or their relatives in other languages) does not reduce to a simple matter of assessing whether what someone *says* is the case actually *is* the case. For that way of putting it already assumes that what is the case is independently given. And that too is a metalinguistic presupposition. Unless we grasp this we shall not understand what was involved in the long Western search for a secure foundation on which to rest logic.

Chapter 5
WORDY REDEFINITIONS

The language connection between philosophy and linguistics in the Western tradition hinges essentially on certain agreements – and disagreements – about the status of words. But here the divinely cathartic question 'What do you mean by that?' must be raised once again.

It is almost impossible to read or talk about language for very long in English without encountering the term *word*. It has long had an established place both in everyday usage and in more technical linguistic treatises. Words, it is commonly assumed, can be uttered, written down, repeated, recorded, and – in literate communities – listed in dictionaries. They apparently have meanings, pronunciations and – in some cases – spellings. A common notion is that language simply *consists in* words and their employment. (One definition of *language* given in the *Shorter Oxford English Dictionary* is: 'Words and the method of combining them for the expression of thought'.) About their existence, consequently, it would seem paradoxical to entertain the slightest doubt. We can sensibly ask when the Prince of Wales's speech is reported, 'What were his actual words?'. (And we would then be nonplussed if told that he did not actually utter any.)

At the same time, it must be pointed out that there are many languages in the world which appear to have no specific term at all corresponding to the English *word*. So it seems in order, if we are to base our metalinguistics on this unit, to ask exactly what that commits us to.

The fact that this common term *word* has such irreproachable metalinguistic credentials has long been a source of embarrassment to those theorists who want to claim that linguistics is a science. For it seems reasonable to ask this science for some account of words. Yet when the question is raised it proves to be unexpectedly difficult to pin down exactly what a word is. Is *she-bear* one word or two? If *can not* is two words, what makes *cannot* one? And then how many are there in *don't*? The word is nothing if not a linguistic unit, but its unity seems puzzlingly elusive. To deny that we use words would be to invite ridicule. On the other hand, to admit that linguists have no better idea than the lay public about what a word is would be to question the credibility of linguistics.

The standard move that linguists make when confronted with this problem is to claim that the word *word* is ambiguous. Since *ambiguity* is itself a second-rank metalinguistic term, this provides a classic example of how, in the Western tradition, metalinguistics comes to its own rescue. Exactly how many ambiguities are involved varies from one theorist to another, but the usual story goes something like this.

'What we utter when, for instance, we ask the way to the station or tell someone what the time is would be a sequence of audible word-forms. But these units are not, patently, the marks on paper that would be produced if anyone were to write down what had been said. Even less are they the units that lexicographers document in dictionaries. Nevertheless, in common parlance these can all be called 'words'. Therefore, it behoves linguistic theory to distinguish at the very least between these three cases. Unfortunately, however, that three-way distinction is complicated by the actual practice of (Western) lexicographers, who introduce a further (metalinguistic) distinction between 'inflexion' and 'derivation'.'

The result of all this can be summarized as follows:

> Standard dictionaries of English (and of most other languages), which are based upon the assumptions of classical grammar, list derivational forms as distinct words, but not the regular inflexional forms, which can be constructed by reference to the 'paradigms' set out in a conventional grammar of the language.[1]

Here metalinguistics comes to its own rescue once more by proposing different terms to correspond to these distinctions. Thus, for example, the term *lexeme* is introduced to replace *word* in those cases where the word in question is a unit of the kind recognized by the lexicographer. Thus the 'lexeme' *sing* is said to subsume such forms as *singing* and *sang* (NB but not *singer* or *song*).

However, it is at just this point in the rescue act that the metalinguistic lifeline starts to fray. A much discussed example of this is Bloomfield's attempt to resolve the problem posed by the gap between the everyday usage of the term *word* and the 'objective' criteria that a science is expected to deploy. His famous definition of the word was 'a minimum free form'. This definition, however, is already several metalinguistic layers deep, and to understand what it says we have to go back to Bloomfield's definition of another common metalinguistic term, *sentence*. The process starts here, with Bloomfield defining *sentence* in terms of *position*:

---

[1]   J. Lyons, *Introduction to Theoretical Linguistics*, Cambridge, Cambridge University Press, 1968, p. 196.

In any utterance, a linguistic form appears either as a constituent of some larger form, as does *John* in the utterance *John ran away*, or else as an independent form, not included in any larger (complex) linguistic form, as, for instance, *John* in the exclamation *John!* When a linguistic form occurs as part of a larger form, it is said to be in *included position*; otherwise it is said to be in *absolute position* and to constitute a *sentence.*[2]

Bloomfield then proceeds to define a *free form.* 'Forms which occur as sentences are *free forms.*'[3] Which is to say that free forms are those which occur in absolute position. Forms which cannot occur in absolute position are *bound forms.* From this, he can move to his ultimate objective:

A free form which consists entirely of two or more lesser free forms, as, for instance, *poor John* or *John ran away* or *yes, sir* is a *phrase.* A free form which is not a phrase, is a *word.* A word, then, is a free form which does not consist entirely of (two or more) lesser free forms; in brief, a word is a *minimum free form.*[4]

Bloomfield makes no bones about condemning the usual 'word' classification adopted by lexicographers and grammarians:

In our school tradition we sometimes speak of forms like *book, books,* or *do, does, did, done* as "different forms of the same word." Of course, this is inaccurate, since there are differences of form and meaning between the members of these sets: the forms just

[2]   L. Bloomfield, *Language*, London, Allen & Unwin, 1935, p. 170.

[3]   *Ibid.*, p. 178.

[4]   *Ibid.*, p. 178.

cited are different linguistic forms and, accordingly, different words.[5]

It is clear from the case he presents that Bloomfield is simply not interested in the lexeme, but has opted for a definition which will identify the word as a certain type of basic segmental unit in the composition of utterances. Before considering what underlies this decision, it may be useful to listen to the arguments of various hypothetical objectors. Some raise objections which Bloomfield had already anticipated.

This is so in the case of Objector 1, who complains that under the 'minimum free form' definition, expressions like *the boy's* and *the king of England's* have to count as single words – which is absurd, since they are patently combinations of words. Bloomfield's reply to this objector is to say that this is a confusion based on 'inconsistencies in our habits of writing'.

> We write *the boy's* as though it were two or three words, but strictly speaking, it is only one word, since the immediate constituents are *the boy* and [-z] possessive, and the latter is a bound form.[6]

Bloomfield has also anticipated the complaint of Objector 2, who urges that *the boy* is plainly a combination of two words. However, it does not count as such under the 'minimum free form' definition, since *the* never occurs in absolute position. Bloomfield's way of dealing with Objector 2 is interestingly different from his way of dealing with Objector 1. Instead of saying that this is just another confusion caused by our spelling conventions, Bloomfield concedes that *the* should count

[5] *Ibid.*, p. 178.
[6] *Ibid.*, p. 178.

as a word, and justifies this by introducing a supplementary criterion of 'parallelism'. He writes:

> The form *the*, though rarely spoken alone, plays much the same part in our language as the forms *this* and *that*, which freely occur as sentences; this parallelism leads us to class *the* as a word:
>
> | | | |
> |---|---|---|
> | *this thing* : | *that thing* : | *the thing* |
> | *this*   : | *that*   : | *(the)*[7] |

It is interesting to ask why Bloomfield adopts this strategy with Objector 2, since it leaves him vulnerable to the criticism that he has already abandoned the 'minimum free form' definition which he proposed only a few moments ago. (This is a point that has actually been raised by some linguists.[8]) Two reasons suggest themselves.

The first hinges on the fact that the only way to count *the* as a word under the 'minimum free form' definition would be to admit a whole range of dubious cases to occurrence in absolute position. 'We can imagine a hesitant speaker who says *The...* and is understood by his hearers.'[9] But Bloomfield doubtless sees that if this counts as occurrence in absolute position, then the theorist is on a slippery slope with nowhere to stop. For then almost any forms or parts of a form could slip through the net and become 'words'.

The second reason is less obvious. Refusal to count *the* as a word would jar not only with lay perceptions of the matter but with the whole European tradition of parts of speech. The article is traditionally recognized

---

[7] *Ibid.*, p. 179.

[8] E.g. Lyons, *op. cit.*, p. 201.

[9] Bloomfield, *op. cit.*, p. 179.

as one of the parts of speech, and forms belonging to all the other parts of speech – nouns, adjectives, verbs, etc. – typically count as 'words'. (As already noted earlier, one of the main interpretations of the parts-of-speech doctrine in the Western tradition is to construe the 'parts' as word-classes.)

Once this is realized, it becomes evident that there is a concealed metalinguistic constraint underlying Bloomfield's different treatment of the two cases. *The* must somehow be brought into the 'word' category, because the article is a part of speech; whereas *the boy's* must at all costs not be resolved into three words, because that would allow a mere inflectional ending (*–'s*) to join the club, and inflexions are not traditionally recognized as parts of speech.

Objector 3, however, takes issue with Bloomfield on a more basic point. 'Where Bloomfield goes wrong,' this objector says, 'is right at the beginning with his account of sentences. For it is perverse to count *John!* as a sentence. *John!* can occur alone simply because it serves as a call to attract someone's attention, or else functions as an exclamation of surprise, remonstrance, etc. But that is not what sentences are. Otherwise *Oh!*, *Ah!*, *Phew!*, *Hey!*, etc., would have just as much right to be included. There are, of course, exclamatory sentences: *What a nice fellow John is!* is one. But *John!* alone just isn't.'

What this objector is objecting to is Bloomfield's lack of respect for the traditional notion that sentences have to say something *about* something (or someone). From this point of view, we are in the domain of sentences if what we say states something about John (*John is a nice fellow*), or proclaims our attitude to something about John (*What a nice fellow John is! If only John were a nice fellow!*), or asks something about John (*Is*

John a nice fellow?), or demands something (*John, be a nice fellow*). But *John!* by itself does none of these things.

It is obvious that what is in train between Bloomfield and these objectors is a metalinguistic battle. In this battle, furthermore, the objectors are defending a traditional metalanguage against a theorist who is intent on proposing certain innovations. Thirdly, however, it is equally obvious that the innovator cannot – for one reason or another – afford to jettison the traditional metalanguage altogether. Thus a theoretical *impasse* is soon reached.

A clue to what is going on – in this as in similar cases – is provided by the innovator's introduction of some new piece of terminology (here *position*). Such innovations are usually introduced in order to bridge a crucial expository or explanatory gap.

Bloomfield's case is particularly instructive. And here we move from the questions raised by Objectors 1, 2 and 3 to that further level of metalinguistic inquiry where the question 'What do you mean by that?' probes the metalanguage itself. *Position* seems a fairly innocuous and perspicuous term; and in that respect Bloomfield's choice shows a certain flair as a linguistic theorist.

But what Bloomfield is doing here is worth careful attention. A traditional lay term (i.e. *sentence*) is being stipulatively redefined in terms which do not feature in lay metalinguistic vocabulary at all. No one – other than linguists – will speak of forms being in 'included position' or in 'absolute position'. But this distinction is introduced by way of a simple example which the lay reader will have no difficulty in making sense of, or in redescribing in non-technical terms. One might say, for instance, that in *John!* the name occurs 'by itself', whereas in *John ran away* it occurs in combination with other words. Bloomfield, however, cannot afford to describe it thus, because he has not yet defined what a word is, and introducing the term *word* at this stage would leave him open to the objection that the whole definitional process leading up to his 'minimum free form' is circular.

Once we grasp what Bloomfield's strategy is, we can see exactly what the metalinguistic role of the terms *included position* and *absolute position* is. They are essential in order to disguise the circularity. Any other two terms Bloomfield might have invented would have done equally well if pinned to the same example. For the interpretation of the example is already guaranteed by the reader's presumed familiarity with the metalinguistic conventions of written English, in which words are separated by visible spaces. But the *utterance* (which Bloomfield claims to be discussing) need not in fact contain any corresponding audible divisions at all. So already we have one sleight of hand from the metalinguistic conjuror, whereby the desired analysis of the example has been slipped into place by substituting consideration of the written form for consideration of the utterance. Without that trick, there is no more reason to split *John ran away* into three than there would be to split *Jonathan* into two.

But the metalinguistic notion of 'position' is doubly suspect. For what it tacitly relies on is a premiss we have already encountered, i.e. that the linguistic sign is linear. In other words, 'position' for Bloomfield is a matter of occurring between two points x and y in a linear continuum. Which in turn, for utterances, involves a correspondence between linearity and temporal succession. But Bloomfield, unlike some other linguists, does not overtly acknowledge this correspondence. In fact, Bloomfield never tells us what 'position' is, other than by giving written examples of the kind cited above.

It is often difficult to realize immediately how many questions are being begged in this kind of manoeuvre. We are only too willing to accept what the printed page tells us (whether in standard orthography or phonetic symbols) as an uncontroversial exposition of the issue. Our typographical innocence attests the extent to which the language professions in Western culture have succeeded over the centuries in bypassing awkward questions about dependence on writing as a technology.

Saussure is the first modern theorist to bring this dependence out into the open. And what Saussure says about reliance on writing can be read as a devastating criticism (in advance) of Bloomfield's whole expository approach:

> It is rather as if people believed that in order to find out what a person looks like it is better to study his photograph than his face.[10]

When he wrote *Language*, Bloomfield had certainly read Saussure; but it is clear that it suited him to ignore Saussure's shrewd observation and use the 'photograph' for purposes of demonstration.

Two further points relating to writing are relevant to the way Bloomfield defines *word* and *sentence*. The first brings us back again to the Bloomfieldian notion of 'position'. One reason why Bloomfield's examples strike his readers as so plausible and unproblematic is that the writing system itself marks the distinctions Bloomfield wishes to make. That is to say, commas, full stops,

---

[10] F. de Saussure, *Course in General Linguistics*, trans. R. Harris, London, Duckworth, 1983, p. 25.

capital letters, etc., leave us in no doubt as to whether a given form is in included position with respect to linearly adjacent forms. But this conveniently disguises the fact that position itself – i.e. linear sequence – does *not* actually do the theoretical job which Bloomfield assigns to it. In order to make it do that job, the assumption has to be made that the linear acoustic sequence is – or may be – punctuated by pauses or silences which somehow mark out linguistic units and structures.

This assumption was explicitly acknowledged by Bloomfield's immediate successors in the field of linguistic theory. Thus Zellig Harris, realizing that it was unsatisfactory to leave the term *utterance* undefined, proposed to interpret it as 'any stretch of talk, by one person, before and after which there is silence on the part of the person'.[11] But this, patently, accentuates rather than solves Bloomfield's problem, because by this criterion an utterance could contain several Bloomfieldian 'sentences'. Charles Hockett went further and proposed to define the term *word* itself by reference to the notion that the linear acoustic sequence is potentially divisible by 'pauses'. His definition runs: 'any segment of a sentence bounded by successive points *at which pausing is possible.*'[12]

This definition, like Bloomfield's, has come in for severe criticism from other theorists, but not always for the right reasons. Thus one critic writes:

> The fact is that speakers do not normally pause between words. Since the native speaker is able to

---

[11] Z. S. Harris, *Structural Linguistics*, Chicago, University of Chicago Press, 1951, p. 14.

[12] C. F. Hockett, *A Course in Modern Linguistics*, New York, Macmillan, 1956, p. 167. Italics in the original.

actualize the 'potential pauses' in his utterances when
he wishes to, even though he does not do this
normally, it follows that the words must be identifiable
as units in his language under the normal conditions
in which he uses it.[13]

But (i) the fact that speakers do not normally pause
between words is irrelevant as an objection, since the
criterion proposed is *potential* pause, and (ii) it does not
follow that the speaker's ability to actualize the potential
pauses presupposes a grasp of prior criteria which are
implicitly operative in the production of speech 'under
normal conditions'. It might be, for instance, that such
an ability depends on the application of a special
technique, which has to be learnt. Thus from the fact
that I can divide a straight line into equal sections if
called upon to do so, it does not follow that the line was
originally drawn as a particular number of equal
sections. In the case of speech, the special technique
involved is clearly writing.

The weakness of the 'potential pause' definition is
more fundamental than these misdirected objections
imply. It resides in the notion of a 'pause' itself. For if
a pause is that which segments a linear acoustic
continuum by interrupting vocalization, then clearly
pauses can occur almost anywhere if the speaker wishes.
But if the speaker decided, for instance, to pause
between syllables, that would subvert the criterion
proposed. In short, the 'potential pause' definition is
latently circular; i.e. the only 'potential pauses' that will
do the trick are those between words.

The second point about writing which is relevant to
defining the word is again one which Saussure picks up

---

[13] Lyons, *op. cit.*, pp. 199–200.

but Bloomfield passes over in silence. The establishment of a fixed written form presupposes that there are already available criteria for deciding which spoken forms can properly be written thus. That is to say, which vocalizations are instances of the *same* word is a problem which drops out of sight as soon as the discussion is conducted by reference to written examples. But, as Saussure points out, the problem, although concealed, remains. For it would be naive to assume that a simple comparison of sounds and meanings will unambiguously identify recurrences. Saussure illustrates his point by asking on what basis we say that in the two sentences *je ne sais pas* ('I don't know') and *ne dites pas cela* ('Don't say that') there occurs the same unit *pas* ('not').

> An idle question, it may be thought. For clearly the identity resides in the fact that these two sentences include the same sequence of sound (*pas*) bearing the same meaning in both cases. But this explanation will not do. [...] It is possible to have an identity without any such correlation. For example, we may hear in the course of a lecture several repetitions of the word *Messieurs!* ('Gentlemen!'). We feel that in each case it is the same expression: and yet there are variations of delivery and intonation which give rise in the several instances to very noticeable phonic differences – differences as marked as those which in other cases serve to differentiate one word from another. [...] Furthermore, this feeling of identity persists in spite of the fact that from a semantic point of view too there is no absolute reduplication from one *Messieurs!* to the next. A word can express quite different ideas without seriously compromising its own identity.[14]

---

[14] Saussure, *op. cit.*, pp. 106–7.

The differences to which Saussure draws attention are, of course, disguised by the uniform spelling *Messieurs!* But the interesting point that is thereby illustrated is that the writing system, by imposing a uniform classification on the varied phonic occurrences, itself plays a crucial metalinguistic role in the whole formulation of the issue.

What Saussure clearly regards as a naive solution to the problem of identifying instances of the same word is, however, exactly the solution Bloomfield proposes. While acknowledging that from a phonetic point of view no two utterances are exactly alike, Bloomfield insists that the linguist has to assume the existence of 'some constant features of sound-wave' which are common to all utterances of the same form. 'Only on this assumption can we account for our ordinary use of language.'[15]

Let us now return to the question of why Bloomfield opts for these definitions of *word* and *sentence*, and engages in a variety of dubious metalinguistic manoeuvres in order to justify them. The reason is that Bloomfield has an ulterior 'philosophical' motive. Bloomfield's agenda is to demonstrate that human language can be explained comprehensively and scientifically on mechanistic behaviourist principles.

In order to carry out this agenda, Bloomfield needs to be able to show that all the terms we need for the analysis of language can in principle be defined by reference to observables. This is what underlies his attempt to define sentences by reference to utterances, and then derive words definitionally from sentences (thus reversing the more usual procedure adopted by Western grammarians, whereby we start from words and explain sentences as combinations of words). The

---

[15] Bloomfield, *op. cit.*, p. 76.

usual procedure will not do for Bloomfield, because the traditional word (= lexeme) is not an observable. It is as simple as that.

* * *

It may be as well at this juncture to forestall some possible misinterpretations. The above criticism of Bloomfield has nothing to do with behaviourism as such. It has no connection with the ritual Bloomfield-bashing that was so popular in the early days of generative linguistics (and is still re-enacted symbolically in the classroom). Behaviourism is here of interest to the present writer simply because it provides a well documented example of a fairly comprehensive attempt to reinterpret the Western concept of *logos* and hence of the role of language in human affairs. That attempt has, to some extent, influenced all subsequent twentieth-century thinking, and the reason for selecting it as an example is that, unlike some earlier movements, it is not so remote from us as to require extensive historical excavation.

The point I wish to illustrate, however, is that *any* thorough-going attempt of the kind that Bloomfield made to reorientate linguistic inquiry inevitably runs up against metalinguistic barriers which require careful negotiation if the attempt is to have any chance of succeeding. It is by studying such negotiations that we can best see where exactly those barriers are placed and how exactly they impede efforts to pass beyond them.

Chapter 6
CONVEYING THOUGHTS

One of the difficulties in the way of producing an unproblematic definition – or redefinition – of the word as a linguistic unit derives from the manner in which the traditional doctrine of the parts of speech dovetails with two other traditional doctrines.

The first of these I will call the doctrine of 'telementation'. Its basic assumption is that communication involves the transference of thoughts from one individual's mind to another's. Words, on this view, are vehicles for thoughts. Speech would be superfluous if human beings were endowed with telepathy. But since we are not telepathic, speech is a convenient and effective way (although by no means the only way) of letting others know what we think.

The other doctrine, which I will call the 'fixed code' doctrine, is that in order to communicate in this way by means of words we have to attach in our minds the same meanings to the same linguistic forms. Thus if I want to let you know what I think of John's behaviour, and say 'John is behaving badly', this will not achieve my communicational purpose if it turns out that you are a monolingual speaker of French and understand no English at all. If, on the other hand, you too are a speaker of English, you will recognize the words I have used and thus be able to understand what I think about John, i.e. that he is behaving badly.

These two doctrines, (i) that speech communication functions telementationally, and (ii) that languages are fixed codes shared by their users, are clearly connected. In effect, (ii) explains how (i) is possible.

Against this background, we can see that the doctrine of 'parts of speech' is only one component in a more elaborate account of how language works. Even in its most primitive version, i.e. from the distinction between *onoma* and *rhema* onwards, the division between parts of speech provides a rough explanation of how we divide up the world mentally in order to communicate thoughts about it. Then, in accordance with (ii), it follows that those who speak the same language will put the parts of speech together in the same way. Otherwise confusion would ensue. For if, say, *Brutus killed Caesar* meant to some people what *Caesar killed Brutus* meant to others, and vice versa, then communication between them, at least as defined under (i), would break down. There would be contradictory reports of who killed whom.

*   *   *

Locke is the philosopher who gives perhaps the clearest statement of this view of language. For him, the basic purpose of language – divinely ordained – is indisputably telementational.

> God, having designed man for a sociable creature, made him not only with an inclination, and under a necessity to have fellowship with those of his kind, but furnished him also with language, which was to be the great instrument and common tie of society. Man, therefore, had by nature his organs so fashioned, as to be fit to frame articulate sounds, which we call words.

But this was not enough to produce language; for parrots, and several other birds, will be taught to make articulate sounds distinct enough, which yet by no means are capable of language.

Besides articulate sounds, therefore, it was further necessary that he should be able to use these sounds as signs of internal conceptions; and to make them stand as marks for the ideas within his own mind, whereby they might be made known to others, and the thoughts of men's minds be conveyed from one to another.[1]

Locke also accepts the reasoning that, in order to fulfil this telementational function, it is necessary that there should be fixed linguistic codes to which the would-be communicators have access in common. For only then will there be any guarantee that the speaker and the hearer attach the same meanings to the same words.

The chief end of language in communication being to be understood, words serve not well for that end, neither in civil nor philosophical discourse, when any word does not excite in the hearer the same idea which it stands for in the mind of the speaker.[2]

Furthermore, for Locke it is obvious that there would be no point in having words with fixed meanings unless people kept to them. Thus for him it is an 'abuse' of language to vary the code, i.e. to use words 'inconstantly'.

Words being intended for signs of my ideas, to make them known to others, not by any natural signification, but by a voluntary imposition, it is plain cheat

---

[1] *Essay Concerning Human Understanding*, III, i, 1–2.

[2] *Ibid.*, III, ix, 4.

and abuse, when I make them stand sometimes for one thing and sometimes for another: the wilful doing whereof can be imputed to nothing but great folly, or greater dishonesty. And a man, in his accounts with another may, with as much fairness make the characters of numbers stand sometimes for one and sometimes for another collection of units: v.g. this character 3, stand sometimes for three, sometimes for four, and sometimes for eight, as in his discourse or reasoning make the same words stand for different collections of simple ideas. If men should do so in their reckonings, I wonder who would have to do with them?[3]

Here it is clear that the requirement (i) that speaker and hearer attach the same meanings to the same words and the requirement (ii) that the speaker attach the same meanings to the same words on different occasions are head and tail of the same coin. Both are necessary conditions for the successful operation of a fixed code.

*   *   *

The same basic model that Locke elaborates in the seventeenth century reappears equally explicitly in twentieth-century linguistics. Locke would have had no difficulty in endorsing in broad outline the account Saussure gives of what he calls the 'speech circuit' (*circuit de la parole*).

The starting point of the circuit is in the brain of one individual, for instance *A*, where facts of consciousness which we shall call concepts are associated with representations of linguistic signs or

[3] *Ibid.*, III, x, 5.

sound patterns by means of which they may be expressed. Let us suppose that a given concept triggers in the brain a corresponding sound pattern. This is an entirely *psychological* phenomenon, followed in turn by a *physiological* process: the brain transmits to the organs of phonation an impulse corresponding to the pattern. Then sound waves are sent from *A*'s mouth to *B*'s ear: a purely *physical* process. Next, the circuit continues in *B* in the opposite order: from ear to brain, the physiological transmission of the sound pattern; in the brain, the psychological association of this pattern with the corresponding concept. If *B* speaks in turn, this new act will pursue – from his brain to *A*'s – exactly the same course as the first, passing through the same successive phases [...][4]

Just as in Locke's scenario, it is evident that, in order to provide an effective means of communication, the 'speech circuit' demands adherence to a fixed code. That is to say, if the concept *B* attached to the sound *A* uttered were different from the concept *A* originally attached to it, there would be a misunderstanding between them. Thus if *A* says *Tuesday*, by this meaning the day that immediately follows Monday, but B, on the other hand, thinks *Tuesday* means 'Wednesday', there is a breakdown in communication. For, according to the telementational model, the concept in *A*'s mind has not successfully been conveyed to *B*'s.

It seems that the main disagreement between Locke and Saussure would concern the *voluntary* character of the process. Locke writes always of individuals *making* signs stand for whatever ideas they please. Saussure, on

---

[4] F. de Saussure, *Course in General Linguistics*, trans. R. Harris, London, Duckworth, 1983, pp. 11–12.

the other hand, seems to regard the speech circuit as working automatically, once activated.

Saussure lays great stress on the fact that individuals do not have it in their power to alter the code (*la langue*).

> No individual is able, even if he wished, to modify in any way a choice already established in the language. Nor can the linguistic community exercise its authority to change even a single word. The community, as much as the individual, is bound to its language.[5]

But perhaps in the end there is no irreconcilable conflict here. Saussure never denies that individuals can lie or cheat. But these, as far as he is concerned, are matters which lie outside the speech circuit as such. Thus for Saussure, Locke's individual who 'makes' a word stand 'sometimes for one thing and sometimes for another' is simply not following the code (*la langue*). The far more important issue on which Locke and Saussure see eye to eye is that *communication*, if it is to be successful, requires speaker and hearer to be (consistently) using the code, i.e. attaching the same meanings to the same words.

*   *   *

However, the Locke-Saussure picture of linguistic communication is to some extent a theoretical idealization, as both concede. Saussure enters the caveat that in practice members of linguistic communities will 'reproduce – doubtless not exactly, but approximately – the same signs linked to the same concepts'. Locke, for his part, is frankly sceptical about whether, in what he

---

[5] *Ibid.*, p. 71.

calls 'civil discourse', communication is reliably established. He discusses at some length the obstacles which stand in the way of individuals ever attaching the same meanings to the same words. He does so because he is primarily concerned to identify the requirements for 'philosophical' discourse (which we might translate nowadays as 'scientific' discourse). In short, he sees the 'imperfections' of words as a major impediment to the establishment and advancement of scientific knowledge.

This, on the other hand, is no concern of Saussure's. Saussure's definition of *la langue* is overtly holistic. The fixed code, as far as he is concerned, is not an assemblage of independently given units, each of which already has a determinate form and meaning. On the contrary, it is the code *in toto* – and the code alone – which confers this determinacy upon its constituent units. Here we see the fixed code taking on a theoretical role which goes far beyond lay conceptions of what 'a language' is. Thus, for the Saussurean analyst, what the lay community regards as one language may well – and almost always will – be a crude amalgam of a number of different languages (or 'idiosynchronic systems', as Saussure calls them), which it is the linguist's job to distinguish.

A no less blatant theoretical extension of the fixed-code doctrine appears in twentieth-century philosophy in the work of Carnap, who proposes to redefine a language as a calculus. Like Locke, he deplores the 'deficiencies' of what he calls 'the natural word-languages' (i.e. languages like English and French). These deficiencies are eliminated from the Carnapian 'calculus'.

By a **calculus** is understood a system of conventions or rules of the following kind. These rules are concerned with elements – the so-called **symbols** – about the nature and relations of which nothing more is assumed than that they are distributed in various classes.[6]

(Carnap, it is worth noting in passing, is wrong about this, i.e. something more *is* assumed from the start; namely, that – as in Saussurean analysis – each element has a determinate form.) The passage quoted continues:

Any finite series of these symbols is called an **expression** of the calculus in question.

The rules of the calculus determine, in the first place, the conditions under which an expression can be said to belong to a certain category of expressions; and, in the second place, under what conditions the transformation of one or more expressions into another or others may be allowed. Thus the system of a language, when only the formal structure in the sense described above is considered, is a calculus. The two different kinds of rules are those which we have previously called the rules of formation and transformation...

This terminology was subsequently taken over in generative grammar by Zellig Harris and Chomsky; and – paradoxically – the whole concept of a 'natural' language as a generative system is borrowed from the sanitized 'artificial' languages which Carnap set up precisely in order to avoid the intolerable 'deficiencies' of the former.

---

[6]   R. Carnap, *The Logical Syntax of Language*, trans. A. Smeaton, London, Kegan Paul, Trench, Trubner & Co., 1937, p. 4.

The function of the 'transformational rules' in the two cases was different but parallel. As far as Carnap was concerned, these were meant to capture what he called the 'logical laws of deduction'. That is to say, the rules stated that if one sentence was composed of symbols combined in a certain way, and another sentence was composed of symbols combined in another (specified) way, then the second can be deduced from the first. Thus the well-formedness of the first guarantees, within the calculus, the well-formedness of the second. Analogously, in early transformational grammar, a correct formulation of, say, the passive transformation, was supposed to capture the fact that if *Brutus killed Caesar* is a grammatical sentence, then *Caesar was killed by Brutus* is too (and similarly for all other pairs of sentences related in this way).

Thus the systematization was conceived no less holistically than in Saussure's case. Indeed, the main complaint that transformationalists brought against Saussure as a linguistic theorist was that he had failed to see or to formalize the combinatorial 'rules' that actually structured *la langue*.

Saussure, for his part, would doubtless have been scandalized by their – and Carnap's – way of proceeding; that is to say, by isolating the formal structure of the system as a separate component. Carnap's calculus – like the early transformationalist's syntactic rules – abstracts from the meaning of the symbols altogether and considers simply their formal relations. In other words, for theoretical purposes, the telementational function of language is deliberately ignored or set on one side. That, from a Saussurean perspective, would have been an entirely retrograde move, a reversion to a more primitive concept of grammar, which fails to recognize that a code has no formal structure *at all* independently of its semantic structure.

It is interesting to note, however, that Carnap goes out of his way to make the point that a calculus, in his sense, is not a system confined to the organization of linguistic expressions. He says:

> the system of rules of chess is also a calculus. The chessmen are the symbols (here, as opposed to those of the word-languages, they have no meaning), the rules of formation determine the position of the chessmen (especially the initial positions in the game), and the rules of transformation determine the moves which are permitted – that is to say, the permissible transformations of one position into another.[7]

This rings a loud bell for anyone who has read Saussure, for chess is the analogy Saussure constantly reverts to when explaining how, in *la langue*, it is the system as a whole which determines the relations between – and the very identity of – the individual units which it comprises. Hence the error to be avoided at all costs in linguistic analysis is the conflation of facts belonging to different systems.

What Saussure would point out about Carnap's invocation of the game of chess is that chess is *not* just a system of pointless combinatorial rules. Nor is it true that the chess pieces 'have no meaning'. Each has a value (*valeur*), and until we grasp what that is we have no idea of what it is to play chess.

*   *   *

Locke, Saussure and Carnap never pursue seriously the problems involved in bridging the gap between their theoretical idealizations and everyday linguistic practice. I am not here proposing to solve these problems for them. If I am right, they are problems that are insoluble, given the way they are set up metalinguistically. I mention them, first, to show that the way they are set up – whether by philosophers or by linguists – itself illustrates how intimate the 'language connection' between philosophy and linguistics in the Western tradition is.

Second, I also wish to draw attention to the fact that, although it actually generates this problem of how *A* and *B* can ever be sure they are attaching the same meanings to the same words, and hence how 'a language' (= code) ever comes into existence in the first place, the telementation-cum-fixed-code model at the same time serves implicitly to validate the metalanguage that the philosopher and the linguist wish to use for their respective purposes. Specifically, it is a model that supports the treatment of speech as involving the recurrent instantiation of a set of units and combinations. In other words, if we look at this strategy with a certain detachment, we see that the problem about how the same meanings get attached to the same words in order to convey thoughts is simply the price that has to be paid (and is paid willingly by both philosopher and linguist) for safeguarding something that is more important to their disciplines, i.e. the metalinguistic framework within which they operate.

Third, although the telementation-cum-fixed-code model is ostensibly brought in to explain the psychological and social functioning of language, it is in any case required by the academic agendas both of philosophy and of linguistics. In short, it answers to a double necessity where these disciplines are concerned.

Let us take linguistics first. Unless languages had fixed forms and fixed meanings, the linguist would be unable to ascertain or describe even the most elementary features of linguistic structure. To see this, it suffices to consider the methodology advocated by Saussure for purposes of linguistic analysis. He provides examples from French which I will not rehearse here.[8] But, essentially, the technique consists in *comparing* one possible segmentation of an utterance with another. The aim of the comparison is to determine which segmentation(s) will allow the analyst to pair up consecutive sound sequences with meanings. The overriding criterion is that the pairing shall leave no residue, i.e. leave no sound which is not accounted for as part of a meaningful sequence, and no meaning which is left unattached to a sound or sounds. Thus, for instance, *Fish swim* will divide into just two such segments (fish + swim) because any less parsimonious segmentation would leave meaningless bits unaccounted for (e.g. *ish*, *sw*, *im*), or else meanings (e.g. 'fish') without a segmentally unitary form.

Clearly, the method Saussure recommends would not be viable unless each utterance were assumed to be structured on the basis of fixed forms and meanings. If, for instance, on some occasions it was the initial segment *fi–* which meant 'fish', but on others the segment *–wim*, then the analysis would collapse. In short, the linguist has to rule out *ab initio* the possibility that the meaning 'fish' is variably distributed over the available sounds, or that – on at least some occasions – it is not attached to any.

For purposes of logic, the assumption of fixed forms and fixed meanings is no less imperative. Take the

---

[8]   Saussure, *op. cit.*, pp. 103–4.

syllogism

1. All men are mortal
2. Socrates is a man
3. Socrates is mortal

The logician would be unable to proceed if *Socrates* in 2 and *Socrates* in 3 were not the name of the same individual, or if *mortal* in 1 and *mortal* in 3 meant something different. These presuppositions are essential to hold the syllogism together.

Whether the above requirements are 'common sense' is not the point. The point is that, whether they are common sense or not (whatever 'common sense' may be), linguistics and philosophy of the orthodox Western variety cannot do without them.

In both disciplines, the overriding priority is internally consistent systematization. Whatever cannot be accommodated and assigned to a determinate place has to be expelled from 'the system'. A sentence which is simultaneously grammatical and ungrammatical is as intolerable to the linguist as an inference which is both valid and invalid is unacceptable to the logician. In both disciplines we see the adoption of a fixed-code concept of languages because *that is what answers to the demands of the theorist* rather than because it corresponds to the observable practice(s) of the linguistic community.

Chapter 7
THE PLAIN TRUTH

The use of the metalinguistic terms *true* and *false* (whatever we take them as properly applying to) cannot be adequately explained on the basis of Saussure's speech circuit. They are terms which presuppose that the speech circuit in turn relates to something else. This relationship we must now examine. But first it is important to be clear about why the speech circuit (or any similar telementational model) will not do the job; for this too is relevant to understanding the incestuous liaison between logic and grammar.

Suppose *A* says to *B* 'Fish swim' and *B* replies 'That's true'. Or suppose *B* says to *A* 'Pigs fly' and *A* replies 'That's not true'. We might imagine either reply amplified in various ways: 'That's true: fish swim.', 'That's true: they do.'; or 'That's not true: pigs don't fly'. Either respondent might go on to cite supporting reasons: e.g. 'Pigs don't have wings'.

Let us now imagine a Martian anthropologist using a recorded corpus of such exchanges as the sole evidence on which to construct a theory about what the Earthwords *true* and *false* mean. The Martian might quite quickly reach the tentative conclusion, on the basis of comparing contexts of occurrence, that these words were antonyms: i.e. that, roughly, *true* meant 'not false' and *false* meant 'not true'. But, in the absence of any positive identification of the meaning of either antonym, this would not be a great step forward.

We will assume that the Martian is working on the general assumption that *A* and *B* use a communication system of the telementational type. His initial hypothesis is that the terms *true* and *false* somehow relate to the cycle of events taking place inside the speech circuit itself. For he observes how frequently *true* and *false* occur in response to what one of the interlocutors has just said, how *true* seems to be associated with a confirmation or repetition of a previous utterance, etc. On this assumption, the best explanation our Martian is likely to come up with is one which defines the words in question in terms of agreement and disagreement between *A* and *B*. Approximately, he will conclude, *true* indicates the speaker's agreement with his interlocutor and *false* a corresponding case of disagreement.

The weakness of this hypothesis is immediately apparent to any Earthling. For while it was perfectly reasonable to conclude that Earthlings *A* and *B* use the words *true* and *false* to indicate their agreement or disagreement *with each other*, what the Martian has apparently failed to realize is that there is another role altogether which these words play. This role has to do with relating messages formulated *inside* the speech circuit to conditions obtaining *outside* the speech circuit. In short, what is missing from the Martian's hypothesis is any recognition of the fact that the speech circuit is not a self-contained enterprise; that when *B* replies, 'That's true: fish swim', it is not simply a question of agreeing with *A*, or of repeating what *A* has just said, but of committing *B* *independently* to the view that, irrespective of this particular verbal interchange, there exist certain aquatic creatures, fish, and that these creatures swim.

The lacuna in the Martian's understanding of Earthspeak is a failure to realize that the speech circuit connects with – and could not work without – what we might call for convenience the 'pragmatic network'. (I borrow the term *pragmatic* from Aristotle's account of the way things (*pragmata*) are linked to words: *De Interpretatione* 16a.) While the speech circuit links *A* to *B* by language, the pragmatic network links both *A* and *B* by language to the world around them. The speech circuit underwrites our use of such metalinguistic terms as *vowel*, *syllable*, *question* and *answer*, while the pragmatic network underwrites our use of *description*, *report*, *fact* and *fiction*.

The point at which speech circuit and pragmatic network intermesh is the *utterance*. The utterance is assessed, as it were, by criteria derived from both. An utterance which leaves us in doubt about what the speaker meant is judged differently from an utterance which leaves us in doubt as to whether what the speaker said is to be believed. But there may be a grey area where these two judgements vie with one another, because it is unclear how to interpret the utterance. The 'ideal' utterance, on the other hand, is one which raises no such problems. As Ruskin once put it, 'the greatest thing a human soul ever does in this world is to see something and tell what it saw in a plain way'. We may perhaps wish to enter a protest about 'greatest', and we should doubtless bear in mind that Ruskin was thinking of art as well as speech; but when due allowance has been made for these reservations, what Ruskin says sums up a set of assumptions which are basic to the whole of Western education. This 'doctrine of plain representation', if we may call it that, is not just a matter of interest to theorists. It arises out of our lay attempts to make sense of our everyday involvement with language and other forms of communication. It affects our assessment of persons as 'honest', 'dishonest', 'reliable', 'unreliable', etc. It supports our notions of what constitutes 'evidence', either formally in a court of law or informally in the transactions of daily life.

The doctrine of plain representation is certainly far older than Ruskin. It is probably, in its most primitive form, coeval with the doctrine of telementation. And in its most primitive form – which still survives in Western discussions of language – it assumes a one-one correspondence between words and what they represent. This notion is captured in the idiomatic expression *to call a spade a spade*, which presupposes that the word *spade* directly and unambiguously designates the tool in question. The implication is that plain speech is speech based on such simple, binary correlations between word and thing. (The doctrine emerges even more perspicuously in the corresponding French expression *appeler les choses par leur nom*: i.e. every 'thing' has its 'name'.) A pragmatic network may be envisaged as the sum total of such word-and-thing correlations underlying the speech of a community.

A pragmatic network, thus conceived, is what links the person Socrates with the name *Socrates,* the colour red with the word *red*, the action of running with the verb *run*. It links them in the sense that the correspondence between the verbal item and its non-verbal partner is an association which apparently makes it possible to proceed with equal assurance from one to the other in either direction. We may start e.g. from the name *Socrates* and proceed to ask which person bears this name; or we may start from the person and ask what his name is. And similarly for colours, actions, etc. These are all metalinguistic inquiries, and the possibility of making them is intrinsic to our everyday understanding of how language works. 'What is this called?' is one of the most fundamental metalinguistic questions. As soon as children can ask it, we feel sure that their feet are already on the path towards becoming fully proficient members of our linguistic community.

To ask 'What is this called?' is, in effect, to ask for information about one particular part of that vast superstructure supported by the pragmatic network. But the child who understands the answer has *eo ipso* understood something about the corresponding speech circuit too. For if this is called x, then A can communicate to B about it by using the expression x. It is in this, at its simplest, that the interlocking of the two consists. Any child who is told that this person is called *Socrates* (or *Bob, Fred, Jim*, etc.), but still fails to see how this information extends the range of what it can now *do* via the speech circuit, (e.g. ask 'Is Socrates alive?', or say 'I don't like Bob') is still, alas, a long way from grasping the opportunities that language affords.

The speech circuit, on this view, is where the action is: it lays out the programme of *how* to do things with words. But *what* you have done or can do by engaging in the speech circuit is determined by the corresponding pragmatic network. A metalinguistic framework structured in this way, i.e. as a speech circuit interlocking with a pragmatic network, prompts the asking of certain questions about language just as surely as it inhibits – or even precludes – the asking of others. Let us first turn to some of the 'askable' questions.

* * *

No one supposes that children are born ready and willing to ask questions like 'Is that true?' or even 'What is this called?'. That would be an absurdity, since such questions must have some verbal formulation; and before they can be formulated the formulator must be presupposed to have acquired the requisite linguistic proficiency. This is the metalinguistic puzzle which underlies the perennial question of the 'origin of language' (at least, as posed within the Western tradition from Plato via Condillac down to the present day).

Thinkers who have tried to tackle this question usually make the standard lay assumptions about how the pragmatic network works. The account runs roughly as follows. Our senses of sight, hearing, touch, etc. acquaint us with things, properties, events, etc. in the world around us. Our vocal organs enable us to make noises. Language is based on our capacity to set up systematic correlations between what we see, hear, touch, etc. and the various sounds and combinations of sounds that we can reliably articulate.

Normally, it is supposed, an individual does not have to establish these systematic correlations from scratch, but simply learns by observation and experiment the correlations already established in the linguistic community. Even this ability, however, is a manifestation of human rationality, of *logos*, and constitutes one of the most important functions of the mind.

Perhaps the earliest explicit description of language-learning along these lines is given by Augustine in Book 1 of the *Confessions*.

> For my elders did not teach me this ability, by giving me words in any certain order of teaching, (as they did letters afterwards), but by that mind which thou, my God, gavest me, I myself with gruntings, varieties of voices, and various motions of my body, strove to express the conceits of mine own heart, that my desire might be obeyed; but could not bring it out, either all I would have, or with all the signs I would. Then, I pondered in my memory: when they named anything,

and when at that name they moved their bodies toward that thing, I observed it, and gathered thereby, that the word which they then pronounced, was the very name of the thing which they showed me. And that they meant this or that thing, was discovered to me by the motion of their bodies, even by that natural language, as it were, of all nations; which expressed by the countenance and cast of the eye, by the action of other parts, and the sound of the voice, discovers the affections of the mind, either to desire, enjoy, refuse, or to avoid anything. And thus words in divers sentences, set in their due places, and heard often over, I by little and little collected, of what things they were the signs, and having broken my mouth to the pronunciation of them, I by them expressed mine own purposes.[1]

Wittgenstein draws attention to this account and makes the following criticism:

Augustine describes the learning of human language as if the child came into a strange country and did not understand the language of the country; that is, as if it already had a language, only not this one.[2]

Wittgenstein's criticism has in turn been criticized. According to Fodor, who holds that 'one cannot learn a language unless one has a language', Wittgenstein was wrong to treat Augustine's account as 'transparently absurd'. On the contrary, 'Augustine was precisely and demonstrably right and seeing that he was is prerequisite to any serious attempts to understand how first

---

[1] *Confessions*, 1, vii. Trans. W. Watts. Loeb Classical Library, London, Heinemann, 1912.

[2] *Philosophical Investigations*, §32.

languages are learned.'[3]   For Augustine was already equipped with what Fodor calls 'the language of thought'.

Unfortunately, neither Wittgenstein nor Fodor seems to have paid very careful attention to what Augustine says in the passage quoted.   There is no ground for attributing to Augustine the bizarre view that he started off with *another* language, and found himself obliged to learn the new language spoken in this strange country populated by adults.   On the contrary, Augustine makes it perfectly clear that his frustration was caused by having no language at all.   What is interesting is that Augustine conceptualizes the problem as *lacking access to the pragmatic network*.

This is also exactly how the problem is conceptualized in Helen Keller's account of her struggles to overcome the limitations of being both blind and deaf.   She is more explicit about the matter than Augustine.   For her, the breakthrough came when she realized that *the things around her had names*.   In her world, the name was not an audible sound sequence but a pattern tapped out by touch.   Nevertheless, this link, once realized, immediately gave her entry to a pragmatic network that would serve as the basis for communication.[4]

In both these accounts, the significant feature is how the sign functions simultaneously as a unit in *both*. Were this not so, learning the correlations with objects would be an idle exercise.   It would certainly not have helped either the infant Augustine or Helen Keller in their attempts to communicate.

Once language-learning is construed in this way, the problem of the origin of language turns into the question

---

[3]   J. A. Fodor, *The Language of Thought*, New York, Crowell, 1975, p. 64.

[4]   H. Keller, *The Story of My Life*, Garden City, Doubleday & Doran, 1902.

of how the correlations were set up in the first place by our remote ancestors, without the benefit of a model to copy. Plato finesses the problem by postulating an original 'name-giver'. In the *Cratylus*, what Socrates, Hermogenes and Cratylus discuss is, mainly, on what principles – if any – the name-giver gave the original names. Cratylus claims – and Hermogenes denies – that 'correct' names have – or once had – a natural connection with what they name.

The point to note for our present purposes, however, is the underlying assumption that *somehow or other* a pragmatic network has to be established in order to act as the basis for a speech circuit. This is also the assumption underlying the Biblical account of Adam giving names to the birds and animals in the Garden of Eden. In both Plato and Genesis, the name-giving is prior to the communicational use of names.

This assumed priority of the pragmatic network over the speech circuit was often taken by later theorists to correspond to a difference between two basic functions of language. One of these functions is social and communicative (served by the speech circuit), while the other is individual and cognitive (served by the pragmatic network). This is what underlies, for instance, Hobbes' metalinguistic distinction between *marks* and *signs*. For Hobbes, marks are words considered in respect of their use in registering our thoughts, observations, etc.; whereas signs are words considered in respect of their use in communicating these thoughts, observations, etc. to others.[5] The same distinction is endorsed today by those generativists who dismiss the communicational role of language as

---

[5]   *Leviathan*, Bk. 1, Ch. 4.

secondary or superimposed.[6] (It makes linguistic theorizing so much easier if there is no need to take society into account.)

A metalinguistic framework of the type described above not only prompts questions about the origin of language and about language-learning but also dictates what will count as acceptable answers. The questions are, in effect, extrapolated from the basic metalinguistic question 'What is that called?' – extrapolated in the sense that from the viability of this question it is assumed that there must, therefore, be general accounts that can be given (i) of binary correlations between linguistic expressions and items or states of affairs in the world at large, and (ii) of how and on what principles these correlations came to be established in the first place.

The only trouble is that this does not follow at all. My view is that the search for such accounts, whether by philosophers or by linguists, is the pursuit of a metalinguistic mirage. What has been overlooked is the fact that 'What is that called?', when uttered as a genuine request for linguistic information, is always a contextualized question. So what 'that' is is contextually identified in some way (perhaps by pointing, perhaps by prior description, or by some other means). This is what makes it possible to give the information requested simply by uttering a word. (*A* asks 'What is that called?' *B* replies 'Hemp'. Or 'Stockbroking'. Or 'Fascism'. As the case may be.) But the simplistic notion that the pragmatic network must therefore be based on some set of binary correlations involves not only generalizing from the original question-and-answer pattern but

[6] See N. Chomsky, *Rules and Representations*, Oxford, Blackwell, 1980, pp. 229ff.

simultaneously decontextualizing the question. Decontextualized, the question no longer makes sense. But it may still look as if it does, if one substitutes for *that* the name of the item in question. Thus the (genuine) information that 'hemp' is what *that* is called becomes, on decontextualization, the trivial truism that 'hemp' is what hemp is called. Just as *a spade* is what a spade is called. Unexciting, but apparently incontrovertible. That is what makes a metalinguistic mirage so convincing, and the doctrine of plain representation sound like undeniable common sense.

*   *   *

How does truth enter the picture? Again, by extrapolation from a very basic metalinguistic question. The question this time is: 'Is that true?'

We see this most directly reflected in the view taken by some philosophers that questions of truth or falsity do not arise at all unless someone *says* something. Hobbes states this assumption as forthrightly as anyone.

True and *False* are attributes of Speech, not of Things. And where Speech is not, there is neither Truth nor Falsehood. *Errour* there may be, as when we expect that which shall not be; or suspect what has not been: but in neither case can a man be charged with Untruth.[7]

Truth is, on this view, a strictly metalinguistic concept. If I believe that the earth is flat, my belief may be mistaken; but until I put this belief into words no question of truth or falsehood arises.

---

[7] *Leviathan*, I, 4.

However, common usage also sanctions speaking of beliefs, impressions, judgements, etc. as being true or false. It could be argued that these cases are merely extensions of a primary concept of truth as applied to what is said. For it has to be possible to express the relevant belief, impression, judgement, etc. as a statement *that* something is the case. Suppose I mistakenly think I saw an elephant at dusk in the garden. My eyesight may be poor, but it is not false. The fleeting visual impression I had may have been illusory, but it was not false. What is false is simply *that I saw an elephant in the garden.*

This extension from the primary metalinguistic usage is the cue for the appearance of the proposition. Propositions appear to be able to do what actual words are incapable of doing; namely, leading a shadowy existence disembodied from any perceptible form. And once this move is admitted, then truth is at last freed from its metalinguistic shackles.

Locke hedged his bets on the issue by recognizing both verbal and nonverbal propositions and, accordingly, what he called 'truth of words' and 'truth of thought'.[8] However, a nonverbal or 'mental' proposition, according to Locke, involves 'a bare consideration of the ideas, as they are in our minds, stripped of names'. This in effect, as Locke admits, presents a serious problem in the discussion of mental propositions, since 'they lose the nature of purely mental propositions as soon as they are put into words'. Furthermore, it is by no means clear what exactly the 'purely mental' equivalent of affirming or denying something is. It might perhaps be argued that my mere

---

[8] *An Essay Concerning Human Understanding*, IV, v.

recognition of a certain colour sample as being red is the mental counterpart of the verbal affirmation 'That is red'. But then it becomes difficult to see how I can mentally deny this; for that would somehow involve 'unrecognizing' or 'derecognizing' what I *ex hypothesi* recognize. (And that difficulty cannot be removed by supposing that I might subsequently take a closer look and decide that it is, after all, not red but purple.)

The variety of solutions that Western philosophers have proposed to the problem of identifying propositions is remarkable and significant. Some have even concluded that the postulation of propositions was a mistake and reverted to treating the sentence as the basic unit for purposes of the systematization of logic. The aim of the present discussion is not to survey, much less to adjudicate between, the various solutions proposed, but to show what the metalinguistic source of the problem is.

If 'proposition' is not a fancy term for 'sentence', what is it? One suggestion is that the proposition is the meaning of the sentence, or at least of the type of sentence that grammarians call 'declarative'. But this will hardly do, for the reason already pointed out by the author of the *Dissoi Logoi*. That is to say, if the grounds for rejecting the sentence are valid (i.e. that the same sentence can be uttered on one occasion to express a truth, but on another occasion to express a falsehood), then the objection must carry over to the meaning of the sentence, unless we are prepared to divorce the meaning from the sentence. But if we do that, we have in effect ushered in two even more mysterious metalinguistic entities, i.e. sentences without (permanent) meanings, and sentence-meanings that float free of their sentences. It is difficult to see where the explanatory gain lies, let alone how the two cohere.

Another suggestion is that the proposition is the *use* made of the (declarative) sentence. Thus if *A* and *B* both utter the sentence *I am an initiate*, they may be said to be putting it to different uses; *viz.* in one case to claim that *A* is an initiate, and in the other to claim that *B* is an initiate. But this does not get us much further either. For all that has been achieved here is the proposal of an arbitrarily restricted employment of the term *use*. When we investigate the nature of the restriction, the 'use' of the sentence turns out to be whatever it is that results in something true or false – e.g. *A*'s claim or *B*'s claim. Here one metalinguistic term (*use*) simply hides behind another (*claim*).

Is the 'proposition', then, more plausibly regarded as *what it is* that is claimed when a claim is made, asserted when an assertion is made, stated when a statement is made, etc.? But here we start another metalinguistic wild goose chase. For *claim*, *assertion* and *statement* are all metalinguistic terms with no better credentials than *proposition* itself. To define the proposition as the 'object' or 'content' of claims, assertions, statements, etc. is simply to substitute one obscurity for another.

Why do these and similar attempts to rescue the proposition all come to grief in this way? Because what is being attempted is a metalinguistic impossibility. The source of the trouble can be traced back to the original culprit, i.e. the sentence, deemed to be unsuitable as the basis for logic. The trouble is that sentences belong to particular languages (English, Greek, Latin, etc.). What the logician seeks to substitute for the sentence is an entity which will afford the same scope for identification, reidentification, generalization and classification, *but independently of the particular languages or words used*. The trouble is that this cannot be done – or at least, not within the Western metalinguistic framework.

For that framework only allows us to identify propositions, statements, assertions, etc. by citing some sentence or part of a sentence.

The moment this strategy fails, any formalization of logic collapses. In other words, the logician cannot, under pain of undermining the whole professional enterprise, claim that there are propositions that cannot be unambiguously expressed in words.

Herculean efforts to move this obstacle merely show how immovable it is. For instance, some theorists have conjured up an entity which is supposed to be what there is in common between an English declarative sentence and its correct translation into any (or all) other language(s). This proposal is either vacuous or circular. For then either there are no propositions at all or else we are off after another metalinguistic will-o'-the-wisp, namely the criteria for 'correct translation'.

*   *   *

Modern proposals to ditch the proposition and resurrect the sentence are no more convincing. Perhaps the most resolute attempt to demonstrate that there actually is a pragmatic network sufficiently robust both to underwrite the sentence and to meet the demands of logic has been made by Quine.[9] Quine begins by cataloguing all the defects that the sentence is heir to. *I am ill* is 'intrinsically neither true nor false', because 'it may simultaneously be uttered as true by one person and as false by another'. *He is ill* fares no better. Even *Jones is ill* presents a similar problem, because 'it is not clear whether "Jones" refers to Henry Jones of Lee St., Tulsa,

---

[9] W. V. O. Quine, *Elementary Logic*, rev. ed., Cambridge, Mass., Harvard University Press, 1966, pp. 5–6.

or John H. Jones of Wenham, Mass.' *It is drafty here* may be 'simultaneously true for one speaker and false for a neighbouring speaker'. *Tibet is remote* is 'true in Boston and false in Darjeeling'. *Spinach is good*, 'if uttered in the sense "I like spinach"' will be 'true for a few speakers and false for the rest'.

The trouble in these cases, according to Quine, is that words like *I, he, Jones, here, remote* and *good* have the effect of 'allowing the truth value of a sentence to vary with the speaker or scene or context'. This will not do for purposes of logic. But what is the remedy? Quine's remedy is verbal surgery. Such words must be cut out and 'supplanted by unambiguous words or phrases'. 'It is only under such revision that a sentence may, as a single sentence in its own right, be said to have a truth value.'

Quine's 'revision' programme, however, immediately runs into metalinguistic problems. The first concerns the notion of revision itself. If we replace, for example, the pronoun *I* by *Henry Jones of Lee St., Tulsa*, or any other explicit identification of the person in question, and alter the verb from *am* to *is* accordingly, it is unclear in what sense we obtain a 'revision' of the original sentence *I am ill*. On the contrary, we now seem to have two different sentences, the only common verbal feature between the original and the revision being the word *ill*. Nor is it clear what is meant by claiming that the revised version, 'as a single sentence is its own right', now has a truth value. What a sentence 'in its own right' is Quine does not explain. Thirdly, it is hard to see how Quine proposes to guard against the possibility that there may be more than one Henry Jones living in Lee St., Tulsa. If the answer is simply that, as a matter of fact, there is only one such person, this is difficult to reconcile with any notion that truth or falsity attaches to the sentence 'in its own right', since the identity of the sentence (however we define it) is presumably independent of the residents of Lee St.

There is a further difficulty with sentences that Quine proceeds to deal with. This is the question of tense. *Henry Jones of Lee St., Tulsa is ill* will be 'true at one time and false at another'. *The Nazis annexed Bohemia* 'was false before 1939 and is true now'. So tenses have to be eliminated as well. This can be done, says Quine, 'by rendering verbs tenseless and then resorting to explicit chronological descriptions when need arises for distinctions of time'. This further revision replaces *Henry Jones of Lee St., Tulsa is ill* by, for instance, *Henry Jones of Lee St., Tulsa is* [tenseless] *ill on July 28, 1940*. Being tenseless, this is allegedly true (or false) 'once and for all'.

But is this curious item retrieved from the timeless permafrost any longer a sentence? No, Quine admits, it is a statement. So what exactly is the relation between it and the sentence *Henry Jones of Lee St., Tulsa is ill* ? The sentence, says Quine, 'uttered as a tensed sentence on July 28, 1940', 'corresponds to' the statement. Unfortunately for Quine's analysis, it also presumably corresponds to a great variety of other 'statements', depending on whether it was uttered at 10am or 5pm, the time zone in which it was uttered, where Henry Jones was at the time, etc.

Quine's final metalinguistic sleight of hand is the proposal that for practical purposes we can go ahead and do logic on the basis of unrevised sentences like *Jones is ill*, provided we bear in mind all the time that we are 'really' dealing with their timelessly unambiguous counterparts.

The sentence is dead: long live the sentence.

Chapter 8
METALINGUISTIC IMPROVEMENTS

So what is the moral of my story? Do philosophers and linguists need to rethink the whole problem of discussing language right from scratch? Certainly they do. Does this require them to construct a new, improved metalanguage which will avoid all the defects of the old one? In order to answer this question, it may be instructive to look at one or two case histories.

An Oxford philosopher was once asked in the heyday of what became known as 'ordinary language philosophy' how, exactly, attention to language helped in understanding problems. He was reported as giving the following answer:

> Suppose I said, 'That chair over there is both red and not red.' This would make you say, 'That can't be right.' Well, I say partly it's the same sort of thing that would make you say 'That can't be right' if you wrote down 'fullfil', spelled f-u-l-l-f-i-l. If you wrote down 'fullfil' that way and you saw it on a page, you would say, 'That can't be right'. Well, this is because you've learned, you see, to do a thing called spelling 'fulfil', and you've also learned to do a thing called using the word 'not'. And if somebody says to you, 'That is both red and not red,' he is doing something that you learned *not* to do when you learned the word 'not'. He has offended against a certain rule of skill (if you like to call it that), which you mastered when

you became aware of how to use the word 'not'.[1]

We might as well begin with this example, because here is as clear a case as anyone could wish of inviting a philosopher with a proclaimed interest in language to explain what the relevance of the study of language is to his professional enterprise.

Let us consider two hypothetical objections that might be made to the philosopher's answer. Both might, conceivably, be made by a linguist. The first objection would be that it is quite misleading to compare the allegedly incorrect use of the word *not* to a spelling mistake. For knowing how to spell is a totally different matter from knowing how to construct sentences. One is a matter of orthography and the other a matter of grammar. To assimilate the two is as misleading as assimilating being able to draw a picture of a bicycle to being able to ride one.

A second objection runs as follows. Saying 'That chair over there is both red and not red' involves an incorrect use of the word *not* is itself a metalinguistic misdescription. For there is nothing wrong with the use of the word *not* in this sentence; nor with that of any other word for that matter. The sentence is perfectly grammatical English. What the philosopher is worried by is something quite different: namely, the apparent violation of the law of the excluded middle. Thus if we remark, as the philosopher suggests, 'That can't be

[1]   V. Mehta, *Fly and the Fly-Bottle. Encounters with British Intellectuals*, Harmondsworth, Penguin, 1965, p. 47. The philosopher in question was R. M. Hare, author of *The Language of Morals*, then a Fellow of Balliol College.

right', that would not be a comment on the use of the word *not*, but on the speaker's apparent commitment to two incompatible claims. The law of the excluded middle is not part of the grammar of English negation, and to suppose that it is would be to confuse syntax with logic.

In both the above cases, what the hypothetical objector is doing, in effect, is defending the domain of the linguist against what is seen as encroachment by the philosopher. And the defence rests on appeal to a traditional metalanguage in which the distinctions which the objector wishes to uphold are already established.

Could the debate between linguist and philosopher be conducted in a neutral metalanguage which contained no built-in advantages to either side? It is difficult to see that it could; for the very terms of the debate arise out of the traditional metalanguage itself.

*   *   *

In this particular instance the issue might, for various reasons, be regarded as not worth pursuing very far. So let us proceed to examine a more robust example of a philosopher making a deliberate appeal to language in the course of presenting a philosophical thesis.

The example chosen for analysis is now sufficiently remote to be considered with a certain historical detachment, but not so remote as to require an effort of historical imagination in order to grasp what it is all about. The year is 1947 and the occasion is Professor A. J. Ayer's Inaugural Lecture on appointment to the Grote Chair of the Philosophy of Mind and Logic at London University.

In this lecture, entitled *Thinking and Meaning*, Ayer attempts to show that what he calls 'the current analysis' of thinking is 'largely mythological'.[2] What immediately follows is my attempt to summarize his paper, with the help of extensive quotations from it.

Ayer begins by outlining a view of thinking which recognizes five essential factors involved.

> There is, first of all, the person who thinks. Secondly, there is the instrument with which he thinks. Normally this is said to be the mind; but it is sometimes reduced to a special part, or faculty, of the mind. In a somewhat different sense, it may be said to be the brain. Thirdly, there is the process of thought itself; and this may be differentiated into various modes. Thus, considering, believing, wondering, doubting, supposing, judging, imagining, knowing, and whatever else may be held to involve thinking in one form or another are brought together under the heading of mental acts. Fourthly, there is the medium in which the thought is carried, which may consist in images but is more likely to be some form of words. And fifthly there is the object of the thought, which is identified with the reference of the images or with the meaning of the words. (p. 2)

In his examination of the five-factor account of thinking, Ayer begins by observing that identifying the fifth factor, the object of the thought, is the occasion for a variety of dubious moves. He argues that since the sentence *It is going to rain tomorrow* has the same meaning whether it expresses a truth or not, what it means cannot be a 'fact' about the world, and someone who thinks that it is going to rain tomorrow cannot have such a fact as the

---

[2] A. J. Ayer, *Thinking and Meaning*, London, Lewis, 1947. All page references are to this publication.

object of the thought. One way round this problem is what Ayer calls

> the invention of propositions, which may either be regarded as altogether distinct from facts, though capable of corresponding with them, or else may be allowed the power of turning into facts, as the occasion arises. (p. 3)

He goes on to point out that one can think of imaginary things, as well as things that are not imaginary in the sense that unicorns are imaginary, but which do not exist in the way that physical objects exist (e.g. numbers, abstractions).

> And the claim that these thoughts too must have their special objects brings in another crop of ideal entities, of which universals are the most notorious. (p. 3)

So although it seems hard to deny that there must be 'something' that the thought is a thought *of*, it proves difficult to say what it is without bringing in a whole retinue of suspect items or processes.

Ayer pursues his attack on the five-factor account of thinking by calling into question factor (ii). He does not deny that we have minds or mental lives, but denies the legitimacy of treating the mind as the instrument with which we do our thinking or feeling. The reason why this role is commonly assigned to the mind is, he suggests, the outcome of a misleading analogy. Because we see with our eyes, hear with our ears, etc., it is assumed that there must be something we think with. But, according to Ayer, neither the mind nor the brain can sensibly be regarded as a thinking-instrument 'in any ordinary sense', even though it may be true that a certain state of our brain is 'a causal condition of our thinking'. It is not, he claims, that thinking is done by some *other* instrument, but that it is not performed *by any instrument at all*.

Following Ryle, Ayer holds that in the cases where a thought is expressed 'the expressing and the thinking merge into a single process'.

> That I converse with a friend intelligently is evidence that I am thinking: but my part in the situation is completely described by saying that I am uttering certain words and also understanding them. The thinking is not a reduplication of the talking: nor, as I shall later try to show, is the understanding a mental act accompanying the words. Admittedly, it often happens that people think before they speak. But, assuming that what they say expresses what they have thought, then all that this comes to is that before saying certain words aloud they say them to themselves. In the one case the words are audible to others besides the person who is using them, in the other case only to himself: but this is not a distinction that affects the present argument. For in neither case is his saying of the words reduplicated by a shadow process of "thought": and indeed the supposition that there are two concurrent processes is even more clearly fictitious in the case where the person "keeps his thoughts to himself" than in the case of his "voicing them aloud." (pp. 7–8)

Having adopted this position, Ayer immediately dissociates himself from 'the notorious behaviourists who have identified thinking with certain movements of the larynx'. For even if it were true that thinking is impossible without laryngeal movements, the former cannot be reduced to the latter. For Ayer the important point is that there are not two processes; a process of using certain words intelligently and a shadow process of "thinking": and this holds equally whether one says the words aloud or says them silently to oneself. (p. 9)

Having rejected this fictitious duality, Ayer returns to the controversial question of 'objects of thought'. He holds that 'it is only through its expression that a thought comes to have an object' and that

the questions whether the thought has an object, and what object it has, are questions about the use of certain symbols, and fundamentally about nothing else at all. (p. 10)

Again,

to say of a thought that it has an object is merely another way of saying that certain symbols are meaningful, and to say what this object is is merely another way of saying what those symbols mean.

(p. 11)

He allows the legitimacy of an extended sense in which we can be said to be thinking about something even when we are not actually using the appropriate symbol (provided we *are* using some other symbol(s) related to it in a certain way).

Thus it might be said that I am thinking of Shakespeare when what I was actually saying to myself was something about the author of Hamlet. In that case what the operative symbol designated would be the author of Hamlet and not Shakespeare: and to this it is no objection that they were one and the same person. For the fact that Shakespeare wrote Hamlet is contingent, in the sense that it would not be self-contradictory, although it would be false, to say that he did not. Consequently, that the author of Hamlet should be Shakespeare is not part of what the expression "the author of Hamlet" means. It follows that in the sense in which to think of an object is to use some symbol which explicitly designates it, what I am thinking of in this instance is not Shakespeare at all but the author of Hamlet. But since it is a fact that Shakespeare did write Hamlet, it comes to be said, in a slightly different sense of the expression "thinking of", that I am thinking of Shakespeare. (p. 11)

An even more degenerate case of an object of thought arises when the symbols actually used 'do not designate anything'.

And by this I mean not that they do not designate anything real, but they may be literally meaningless.
(p. 12)

Thus a mystic may claim that 'the Absolute transcends human reason' and intend this to have a meaning

even though he cannot explain what it means, and indeed, strictly speaking, does not himself succeed in attaching any meaning to it. We may say then that sentences of this sort express quasi-propositions; and if a sign is such that it has a place only in sentences of this sort we may describe it as a quasi-symbol. Furthermore these quasi-symbols have their equivalents, inasmuch as the sentences in which they occur can be translated. That is to say, the quasi-propositions which they express can be expressed by other sentences, whether of the same or of a different language. And what passes as the designation of a quasi-symbol and so comes to be regarded as a possible object of thought, is just the quasi-symbol itself, or one of its equivalents. (pp. 12–13)

Fourthly, Ayer allows 'objects of thought' that are not designated by any symbol the thinker is using at the time, but which are 'logical constructions' out of objects so designated.

> It is in this sense, for example, that I may be said to be thinking about philosophy, even though I do not use any symbol that explicitly designates it. For to practise philosophy is just to use and understand a certain class of sentences, and the sentences that I am using are members of this class. (p. 13)

Ayer's comprehensive definition of an object of thought thus has four clauses:

> *A* is thinking of *x* if and only if either (1) *A* is using certain symbols of which at least one designates *x*, or (2) there is a *y* such that *A* is using certain symbols of which at least one designates *y*, and it is a fact that *x* is *y*, or (3) '*x*' is a quasi-symbol and *A* is either using '*x*' or some quasi-symbol which is equivalent to '*x*', or (4) there are *y*, *z*... such that *A* is using certain symbols which designate *y*, *z*... and *x* is a logical construction out of *y*, *z*.... (p. 13)

Ayer holds that usually we do not think of something unless we are thinking something *about* it. This does not necessarily involve *believing* the thought we are entertaining. Nevertheless, in these cases too what the thinker is thinking

> may be expressed by a sentence; and what makes his thought a thought *of* something is simply the fact that this sentence has a meaning. (p. 14)

Ayer's alternative to the mistaken view that there are specific mental acts designated by specific mental terms is that the terms in question designate dispositions.

In their ordinary usage, indeed, such words as "knowing" or "believing" or "doubting" are dispositional words; and to say of someone that he knows, or believes, or doubts something is not to say that he is *doing* anything at all. (p. 14)

The difference between e.g. believing and doubting

is a difference of disposition: it is a difference in what I am disposed to say on the relevant occasions, in the way in which I am disposed to say it, and in the actions that I am disposed to take. (p. 15)

For Ayer,

p enters into the fact that *A* believes that *p* only in so far as the statement that *A* believes that *p* is a statement about language. In so far as it is not a statement about language, but a statement about the person *A*, then *p* does not enter into its analysis at all. (p. 17)

Having thus appealed to language in order to undermine the credibility of mental acts, Ayer turns to deal with the objection 'that the use of symbols which are meaningful is itself just such a mental occurrence as I am trying to eliminate'. The objection, as Ayer concedes, is not easily disposed of.

What is true is that if I am to understand a symbol, I must, in some sense, know what it stands for. But my knowing what it stands for does not imply that I am actually imagining anything, or indeed that anything is going on "in my mind." It is, if you like, a matter of my being familiar with the symbols in question; but this familiarity is purely dispositional. In the case of an empirical statement it is a matter of my being able to describe, and ultimately to recognize, the situations that would make it true. And this ability to describe or recognize is not something that I actually have, like a cold in my head, or a shilling in my pocket. I have it only in the sense that I should behave in the appropriate way if the appropriate occasions arose.

(pp. 21–2)

Ayer rejects the explanation that knowing what a class-symbol stands for is a matter of familiarity with the corresponding universal.

> It is not *because* I am familiar with the universal "manhood" that I am able to think, or to talk intelligently, about men. My familiarity with this universal just consists in the fact that I am able to use the word "man" correctly. And what is meant by my using the word correctly is, first, that I adhere to the conventions which determine the possibilities of its combination with other words, and secondly, that I apply it to the appropriate situations. (p. 24)

Finally, Ayer contends that 'to say of a symbol that it has a meaning is not to say that there is something that it means' (p. 25). More generally, he rejects the idea 'that meaning is a relation which holds between a symbol and some other term' (p. 26), and holds that 'to say what a symbol means is not to relate it to an object, but to give it an interpretation in terms of other symbols' (p. 27). The problem of truth is, accordingly, 'a semantic problem' (p. 27).

> Thus, "Napoleon lost the Battle of Waterloo" is true if and only if Napoleon lost the Battle of Waterloo. We can say, if we like, that the words "Napoleon lost the Battle of Waterloo" express the proposition that Napoleon lost the Battle of Waterloo, and that this

proposition is true because it corresponds to the fact that he did lose it. But if, as is commonly done, we generalize this by saying that sentences express propositions, and that propositions are true when they correspond to facts, we are liable to fall into confusion. For apart from the awkward questions which this formulation tends to raise about the status of propositions, it also leads people to suppose that truth is a matter of accurate photography, and that facts are objective entities eternally posing for their photographs.

(p. 28)

Nevertheless, semantics is not a matter of endless referral from one symbol to another. It is not the case

that we are imprisoned in language, as some philosophers have supposed. For in the end we verify the proposition not by describing, but by having, an experience. We interpret one symbol by another; but it is only because this circle is broken by our actual experiences that any descriptive symbol comes to be understood. (p. 28)

This assertion concludes the lecture.

*   *   *

Whatever one thinks of the cogency of Ayer's arguments, it is clear that the appeal to language not only spearheads an attack on mental acts, but ends up underwriting a general theory of truth. (For this, Ayer is heavily indebted to Tarski, but it is a debt which, in this particular lecture, he curiously fails to acknowledge.) What Ayer is trying to do – whether successfully or not – is of considerable interest for our present purposes. It is to resolve an ancient philosophical problem which is central to the language connection. It concerns the relationship between speech and *logos*.

Although Ayer describes his target as 'the current analysis' of thinking, it is significant that this current analysis is strongly supported by traditional ways of talking about language. To speak intelligently and intelligibly, it is widely supposed, is a matter of putting your *thoughts into words*. And that is taken to involve *choosing* the words which fit the thought you wish to *express*. If you choose the wrong ones, then those words will not express what you *meant* to say. So in denying that there is any separate process of thinking, Ayer is in effect up against a common way of describing and considering the whole speech process.

Ayer does not say what he takes the connection to be between 'the current analysis' of thinking and those forms of common parlance which seem to imply that the analysis is correct. He does not claim that anyone has been 'misled' by language here, or that these are what Ryle called 'systematically misleading expressions'.[3] Nevertheless, part of Ayer's expository problem in this lecture is that he is having to struggle against the kind of terminology which supports unreflecting acceptance of the dichotomy between *thinking* and *speaking*. In denying that our thinking goes on independently of and prior to our use of words, he has to take care not to sound as if he is just talking nonsense. (He may not always succeed, but that is a different matter.)

Let us now listen to the complaints of the following hypothetical objectors. All of them could be linguists, but it is not essential that they should be thus identified.

---

[3] G. Ryle, 'Systematically misleading expressions'. Reprinted in A. G. N. Flew (ed.), *Logic and Language*, Oxford, Blackwell, 1951.

Objector 1 asks what Ayer can possibly mean when he says that in cases where a thought is expressed, 'the expressing and the thinking merge into a single process'. Ayer presents this as 'a less radical thesis' than claiming that the process of thought is indistinguishable from the expression of it, although he is 'inclined' to believe that the more radical thesis is also true. But, pursues the objector, it is at least reasonably clear what the more radical thesis claims; namely, that the properties of the thought process and the properties of its expression cannot be differentiated. And this is patently false. (Were it true, there would be no way of describing an utterance without *eo ipso* describing what it meant.) But we cannot so easily dismiss the less radical thesis, precisely because it is entirely obscure. To speak of 'merging' normally presupposes two previously distinct things or activities which come together as one (e.g. rivers, companies, cultures). But if this is how we are to interpret 'merging' here, it undermines Ayer's own claims; for what Ayer is at pains to deny is the existence of two separate things or activities. If there were never *two* in the first place, how could they merge? Ayer is thus trapped by his own metaphor.

Moreover, the objector continues, even if Ayer responded by withdrawing the metaphor, we would have the right to ask what Ayer was thinking when he used it. Was it an unfortunate choice of expression, which did not really express what he thought? But if so, we are back with a divorce between the thinking and the expressing. Or are we to suppose that Ayer thought what he said, i.e. that two separate processes merged. In which case, what he said (and thought) conflicts with his own case. Metaphor in general is a difficult linguistic phenomenon for Ayer's theory to handle. The standard explanation of it, dating back to Aristotle, involves supposing that you can say one thing and mean another. (Irony is another fish from the same kettle.)

But other linguistic phenomena which Ayer seems to have overlooked are no less difficult. For instance, if I utter an ambiguous sentence, do I have an ambiguous thought? Or, worse still, am I then incapable of deciding which of the two possible thoughts I am actually entertaining. Presumably not. I may not even realize the ambiguity. But then there must be some selection process Ayer has not told us about which sorts the matter out. The *sentence* does not do that job for us, since *ex hypothesi* it leaves the ambiguity unresolved. Ayer, indeed, seems to ignore or be insensitive to the distinction between sentences and utterances. If I say to myself *This chair is uncomfortable* I am, according to Ayer's theory, having a certain thought about the chair; but presumably if I then sit in another chair and say to myself *This chair is uncomfortable*, I am having a different thought. For although the question of comfort arises in both cases, the chair in question is different. Yet the sentence *This chair is uncomfortable* does not distinguish the two thoughts. How could it? For it is a sentence which has to do for thoughts about indefinitely many chairs on indefinitely many occasions.

In brief, Ayer's insistent denial that there are 'two concurrent processes' not only leads him into what is tantamount to self-contradiction but grossly oversimplifies the complexities of language. It is precisely to take account of those complexities that we tend to separate out, in our discussion of these matters, the thinking process from the speaking process. Conflation of the two is all that Ayer's theory achieves.

How might Ayer respond to this objector? He might just concede that the merging metaphor was a tactical mistake. But the rest requires something more convincing than graceful withdrawal, and the two obvious moves available are both unsatisfactory. He could conceivably agree that the English language provides for only one possible thought to be expressed by the sentence *This chair is uncomfortable* and that whenever this sentence is used, the thought is exactly the same. But then he seems to have failed to capture the sense in which it is important for me to be able to distinguish separate chair-thoughts: e.g. if I am going to call in an upholsterer, it is important to know *which* chair I think uncomfortable.

The alternative move Ayer might make is to choose to say that such a sentence as *This chair is uncomfortable* changes its meaning with different circumstances of utterance. But to make that move, the objector will point out, is to admit that there is an important non-verbal component to the meaning. In short, whether Ayer goes for the sentence-meaning or the utterance-meaning, it is far from clear that the words alone can do the job Ayer's theory requires, i.e. identify the 'object of thought'. And if this is so, it follows that Ayer has failed in his attempt to eliminate mental acts from his account of thinking.

Objector 2 simply asks what Ayer means by the term *disposition*. Ayer's paper introduces 'dispositions' as the key to behaviour, including linguistic behaviour. Linguistic knowledge is explained as a set of dispositions to use words in certain ways. But is a disposition different from a habit? Or from a trait, an inclination, or even a tendency? We are not told. The suspicion is that Ayer is using *disposition* as a convenient cover term for a mechanism with a deliberately vague explanatory role. In which case, dispositions are no less a theoretical figment than mental acts. Like the latter, they are not open to inspection. At best they are inferred from what people do and say. But so are mental acts. So – the objection runs – all Ayer's theory does in the end is substitute one unobservable (the disposition) for another (the mental act). It is not clear that very much has been gained. Furthermore, it is simply question-begging to assume the validity of a dispositional theory of linguistic knowledge in the absence of any detailed account of the dispositions. For instance, I may think I know the meaning of the English numerical expression *ninety-nine* but be a complete duffer at arithmetic. Does e.g. the fact that I am often disposed to use the term *ninety-nine* when the correct answer should be 'ninety-eight' or 'a hundred and one' show that my knowledge of English is defective? More generally it would seem that Ayer would have to maintain that knowing the same language as another person must be reducible to having the same dispositions with respect to the use of words. But, manifestly, all speakers of English do *not* have the same (verbal) dispositions: on the contrary, they often argue over words, as indeed Ayer himself is doing in his lecture.

Objector 3 asks what Ayer means when he says that 'in their ordinary usage' *knowing, believing* and *doubting* are 'dispositional words'. If this is a claim about English, there is a singular lack of linguistic evidence for it. We do not, for instance, regularly explain or paraphrase statements about what people know or believe or doubt by substituting statements about their dispositions. (Cf. *He knows how much money he has in the bank* = ?*He is disposed to act in such-and-such ways regarding the amount of money he has in the bank.*) Nor vice versa. (Cf. *He is generously disposed* = ?*He knows (believes, doubts...) certain things about generosity.*) On the other hand, it makes perfectly good sense in English to paraphrase cognitive verbs in terms of mental acts or states. (E.g. *I don't know whether it is going to rain or not = I am uncertain whether it will rain = I cannot make up my mind about whether rain is likely.*) Ayer does not even recommend that we should pay careful attention to the ways in which cognitive verbs and ascriptions of dispositions are actually used in English. Yet his conclusions seem to imply that a lexicographer who supplied a mental-act definition of a cognitive verb would actually be misdescribing the 'ordinary usage' of the word in question.

Objector 4 asks what Ayer means by drawing a distinction between symbols and quasi-symbols. For his definition of the neologism *quasi-symbol* is incoherent. But it is not irrelevant to his argument, because it features in clause (3) of his comprehensive account of the 'object of thought'. All Ayer tells us is that a quasi-symbol is one occurring only in sentences which express quasi-propositions: it is 'literally meaningless'. This seems to suggest that a quasi-symbol is something other than a word like *unicorn*, which merely designates something which does not exist. For the word *unicorn* can occur in perfectly sensible sentences, e.g. *Unicorns do not exist.* But then we wonder if there are *any* words which could ever meet the conditions Ayer stipulates, i.e. being meaningless and occurring *only* in sentences expressing quasi-propositions. The sole example Ayer provides is the word *Absolute*, as in *The Absolute transcends human reason*, and the only reason he gives for refusing to count this as a symbol is that 'no symbol designates the Absolute'. But how Ayer can be sure of this he does not tell us. If it is simply that there is no such thing to be designated, then it falls into the same category as *unicorn*. But *unicorn*, as already noted, does not seem to qualify as a quasi-symbol. In short, Ayer's invention of the neologism *quasi-symbol* is an obfuscation brought in to cover his reluctance to come straight out and assert that those who express themselves in mystical, arcane, hermetic or enigmatic language are not thinking at all. (This presumably applies to a considerable number of philosophers, from Pythagoras onwards.)

Objector 5 asks what Ayer means when he says that truth is 'a matter of establishing a set of semantic rules'. For while there are lexicographical definitions for the words *truth*, *true*, *truthful*, etc., it would be a confusion to suppose that these supplied rules for using all the other words in the vocabulary in such a way as to express truths. More generally, it is absurd to suppose that the rules of English (or any other language) supply truth-conditions for the *application* of all English words. Ayer here seems to be conflating linguistic knowledge with knowledge of – or judgement about – the world. If *A* and *B*, in possession of the same evidence, disagree about whether it is true that *C* is guilty, this does not mean that one or other does not know the meaning of the word *guilty*. All that is needed to account for the divergence is that they differ in their assessment of the case. (Otherwise, jury disagreements would be prima facie evidence of the linguistic incompetence of the jurors.)

Objector 6 asks what Ayer means by the term *designation*. For this is very relevant to the way he draws the distinction between clauses (1) and (2) in his definition of an object of thought. For Ayer, evidently, it is obvious that the expression *the author of Hamlet* does not designate Shakespeare. But, unless the term *designate* is being used in some special way here, it seems difficult to deny that the expression *the author of Hamlet* can be so used, and often is. For example, a literary critic writing about the life and works of Shakespeare may, simply for reasons of stylistic variation, sometimes refer to the bard by name and sometimes as *the author of Hamlet*. It would be absurd for readers to suppose that when this change occurred in the text a different person was designated. On the other hand, if the critic is actually contesting Shakespeare's authorship of Hamlet, it may well be that the reader is expected to understand that the terms *Shakespeare* and *the author of Hamlet* are *not* to be taken as designating the same person. Which is the case depends on the context. We cannot settle the matter by staring hard at the four words *the author of Hamlet*.

Moreover, this objector continues, is it indeed a 'fact' that Shakespeare wrote Hamlet, as Ayer seems to assume? Surely the truth or otherwise of the statement 'Shakespeare was the author of Hamlet' depends rather crucially on the designation of the name *Shakespeare*. But here we seem to be going round in a circle. Do facts come first or designations?

This links up with a problem about the difference between clause (1) and clause (2) of Ayer's definition. The latter reads:

> there is a y such that A is using certain symbols of which at least one designates y, and it is a fact that x is y. (p. 13)

But this will hardly do unless the 'fact' is *known* to or *assumed* by the thinker. For it would be extremely odd to maintain that someone who uses the expression *the author of Hamlet* is thinking about Shakespeare if that person actually at that time thinks the author of Hamlet was someone else. The reason why Ayer is unwilling to insert this proviso, however, is clear: to do so would be to reintroduce precisely the kind of cognitive act or state that his account endeavours to eliminate.

Now all the arguments that Objectors 1–6 bring against Ayer are essentially metalinguistic arguments. In effect, what the objectors are doing all the time is defending a traditional metalanguage against Ayer's attempts to tamper with it. They are spelling out, against Ayer, the implications of that metalanguage. And Ayer's position is weak or difficult to sustain precisely because, although he is clearly sceptical about the value of certain parts of the traditional metalanguage (e.g. the term *proposition*), although he is prepared to introduce new metalinguistic terms of his own (e.g. *quasi-symbol*), and although he seems to want to redefine others (e.g. *designation*), nevertheless at the end of the day he is committed to stating his case within the framework of that traditional metalanguage. For he actually needs some of its very basic terms (e.g. *word*, *sentence*, *meaning*) in order get his argument off the ground.

Where the objectors have the rhetorical edge over Ayer is that, unlike him, they have no ulterior agenda which leads them to want to question any part of the metalanguage at all. If what underlies it is the very distinction between thinking and speaking that Ayer rejects, that does not worry them in the slightest. They use the traditional metalanguage against Ayer to try to show that his position is unacceptable and his claims either obscure or nonsensical. In other words, they are prepared to raise the metalinguistic question 'What do you mean by that?' *on the assumption that* any acceptable answers have to be formulated in the traditional metalanguage itself, or in terms compatible with it. Their bottom line is either 'You can't expect us to reject p', where p is couched in impeccable metaspeak; or else 'You can't expect us to accept q', where q involves a metalinguistic innovation of Ayer's.

Again, there is no way this kind of debate can be settled. Proposing an improved metalanguage offers no solution, since what will then be called into question sooner or later is whether the supposedly better metalanguage is any improvement at all. (This fate has in recent years overtaken various metalinguistic innovations proposed by linguists in the name of 'advances' in linguistic theory. The twentieth-century casualty list now includes *phoneme, morpheme, transformation, deep structure*, and many more.)

It is ironical that Ayer goes out of his way to deny 'that we are imprisoned in language'. For the metalinguistic difficulties he has in presenting his own case suggest that, if not imprisoned, the philosopher is at least under house arrest.

In short, it seems that linguistic inquiry in Western culture is locked into a metalinguistic framework which is highly resistant to basic change, even though its presuppositions are extremely dubious and easily shown to be so. Nevertheless, the survival of this framework undoubtedly serves a purpose. It underwrites the continuity of both philosophy and linguistics as academic disciplines. It articulates the relationship between them and validates their own dependence on language in pursuit of traditional disciplinary objectives. It allows a certain range of linguistic questions to be raised and debated, while precluding the acceptance of any fundamentally radical answers. Thus it functions rather like a political theory of which the underlying purpose is to justify and preserve existing institutions, while permitting a limited degree of freedom in proposing possible improvements to them.

What the sceptic will conclude from all this is that it is no use trying to tinker with the underlying metalinguistic framework. The alternatives are not acceptance-with-modifications versus unqualified acceptance. The alternatives are simply acceptance versus rejection. But if the acceptance is not to be ostrich-like, and if the rejection is to be constructive rather than a gesture of defiance or a mere reaction of despair, we have to be clear about where the basic faults in the framework lie.

Chapter 9
METALINGUISTIC MISTAKES

Anyone who says that *treize* is the French word for 'fifteen' is making a metalinguistic mistake; but it is a fairly trivial one, easily corrected, and the sense in which it *is* a mistake is unproblematic. To say that a metalinguistic term itself is wrong is a more complicated case. It might, for instance, be argued that the Greek term *stoikheion* for the minimal linguistic unit must be rejected because it conflates letters with sounds. Or it might be held that the recognition of so-called *zero* elements in linguistic analysis (as in the plural of *sheep*) is theoretically objectionable. Again, although the issues are more contentious, it is not difficult to see what the alleged mistake is.

But there is a third kind of metalinguistic error which is altogether more difficult to get to grips with. There are cases in which a metalanguage as a whole, or some substantial part of it, is inadequate or potentially misleading. And this, I believe, is the kind of case we are dealing with in the Western tradition.

In general, there seems to be no reason to deny the possibility that words may reflect mistaken beliefs about the world or errors in human perceptions of it. On the contrary, the theme has been a familiar one in Western philosophy at least since Bacon, whose famous 'idols of the market' are due to expressions which mislead human judgement because they are based on and perpetuate erroneous assumptions.[1] Hobbes warns that language may be a source of self-deception: men 'register for their conceptions, that which they never conceived; and so deceive themselves.'[2] Locke devotes a whole chapter of the *Essay Concerning Human Understanding* to the 'imperfection of words' and another to the 'abuse of words'.[3] A further level of error arises when words generate questions which appear to be about matters of substance, but which are themselves merely verbal disputes. Hume regards being confused on this level a fault to which philosophers are particularly prone.

> Nothing is more usual than for philosophers to encroach upon the province of grammarians; and to engage in disputes of words, while they imagine that they are handling controversies of the deepest importance and concern.[4]

But even if individual terms can mislead in this way, could a whole area of human vocabulary and the discourse based upon it be thus flawed? Again, there seems no general reason to deny this. Arguably, at various times and places in the world, the language of cosmology, geography, medicine, and religion has been deeply flawed for precisely this reason. It should be noted that in such cases the underlying mistaken assumptions, although they may generate apparently sensible but actually unanswerable questions, do not automatically impede the collection and systematization of accurate information. And this in itself may reinforce

---

[1]   *Novum Organum*, trans. J. Devey (*The Physical and Metaphysical Works of Lord Bacon*, London, 1853), I, xliii.

[2]   *Leviathan*, I, 4.

[3]   *Essay*, Book III, Chs. 9 and 10.

[4]   *An Enquiry Concerning the Principles of Morals*, §261.

confidence in the discourse as a whole. Thus if you believe that the earth is flat, you may waste a great deal of time puzzling about what the underside is like, but that need not prevent you from making a reasonably good map of the surface you can see. The problems will come only at the point where you try to mount an expedition to explore the underside, or put all your separate topographical observations together and *interpret* them as a comprehensive description of a flat surface. You will then find that there seem to be unexplained contradictions in your measurements.

If it is granted that whole areas of inquiry and the terminology that goes with them may be mistaken in ways such as these, it seems difficult to reject out of hand the possibility that an entire metalanguage might be similarly mistaken. Presumably, the risk in such a case would be that the flawed metalanguage would generate a whole range of misconceived questions about language itself. How might this come about?

Let us begin by trying to imagine a metalanguage which simply does not permit the kind of discussions that were reviewed in the preceding chapters. In this language we find no terms remotely comparable to those in which the debates between Ayer, Bloomfield and their critics were conducted. This is not to suppose that the people who speak this language never have occasion to discuss speech. On the contrary, their metalanguage might be extremely rich; but it might embody quite different conceptions of what is going on in the typical act of speech from those which underlie Western metalanguage.

Let us suppose the metalinguistic account might be summarized as follows. Each utterance begins within the body of the speaker as a quantity of fluid secretion. This is warmed in the liver by heat from the heart. The heated verbal fluid turns to vapour, which is expelled by the lungs, and then acquires acoustic properties in virtue of the action of the larynx, tongue, palate, lips and teeth. Good speech is expelled by filling the right lung followed by the left lung, and bad speech *vice versa*. This pulmonary process gives the expelled vapour a characteristic spiral rotation. The rotating vapour is trapped in the ear of the hearer, whence it is transferred to the hearer's larynx, condensed into liquid, and swallowed. The liquid has various properties depending on the vapour rotation, which in turn was determined by whether the speech was good or bad. In the case of good speech, the swallowed liquid in the hearer's body refreshes the heart and nourishes the liver. In the case of bad speech, the swallowed liquid dries and heats the heart and contracts the liver. The liver rejects the verbal liquid from bad speech and passes it on to the spleen: it darkens the spleen and causes various kinds of physical discomfort. (Women, who are held to have delicate livers, are most easily hurt by bad speech.) In the case of good speech, the intestines 'digest' the verbal fluid, extracting the nutritive elements from it, and distributing this nutrition to other parts of the body. Good speech is thus 'food' for the hearer.

Now in fact the above account is by no means entirely fictitious. It corresponds fairly closely to the metalanguage of the Dogon people of West Africa, studied by Calame-Griaule.[5] But for our present purposes it would make no difference if it were simply hypothetical, so let us call it just 'the D-account'.

---

[5]   G. Calame-Griaule, *Ethnologie et langage. La parole chez les Dogon*, 2nd ed., Paris, Institut d'Ethnologie, 1987.

Now the D-account is quite comparable to – although in detail quite different from – the kind of account of the speech act that we encounter in Western linguistic theory. Saussure's 'speech circuit' (see Chapter 6) tells us a story about an utterance beginning in the brain of the speaker, which possesses a store of atomic units called 'concepts', and another store of units called 'sound patterns'. These in turn consist of sequences of atomic units which 'represent' individual sounds. Concepts and sound patterns are already paired in one-one or one-many correspondences. Speech, according to this account, involves, in the simplest type of case, the activation of one of the concept units in the brain, which 'triggers' the corresponding sound pattern. This pattern in turn passes a 'message' to the speaker's organs of phonation (larynx, tongue, lips, etc.). The organs of phonation receive this neural message and take appropriate physiological action, initiating muscular movements which cause air vibrations of a specific complex form. These forms are already paired in one-one correspondence with the sound pattern units. The vibrations are transmitted through the air to the hearer's ears. There they are transformed into neural impulses which send a message to the hearer's brain. This message identifies and activates one of the stored sound patterns in the hearer's brain, which in turn 'triggers' the concept paired with it. The hearer already has an identical store of concepts to that possessed by the speaker. When the concept triggered in the hearer's brain matches the concept originally activated in the speaker's brain, the speech act is successfully completed and the hearer has 'understood' the speaker.

Although first stated in roughly the above form by Saussure, this represents a view with a very long history in the Western tradition. (Essentially similar analyses are offered by other writers, some more fully elabo-rated.[6]) Let us call this the E-account.

In both the D-account and the E-account, we are dealing with a process which may be directly relevant only to a small subset of the total number of terms in the metalanguage. But it provides a scaffolding for much more and already reveals a basic difference between the two cases. In the E-account, speech is viewed exclusively as an intellectual transaction, as the handing over of an abstract item of information. In the D-account, on the other hand, speech is viewed much more 'physically', as something one person *does* to another person's body.

There is much more to Dogon metalanguage than is represented in what I am calling the D-account. But, as Sylvain Auroux points out, a European will doubtless find the whole Dogon way of talking about language puzzling until it is situated in the wider context of beliefs and practices typical of Dogon culture.

> Expressions – ways of speaking – are classified in terms of their role in myth and according to a system of symbolic correspondences linking them to a technique, an institution, a plant, an animal or a part of the human body...
>
> If the Dogon talk about language in a complex and codified way...it is not so much that they distinguish between symbolism and reality as that, for them, the whole of reality is symbolic. The words a man exchanges with his wife before having sex are considered as being 'good' or 'bad'; they join with

---

[6] E.g. P. B. Denes and E. N. Pinson, *The Speech Chain*, Garden City, N.Y., Anchor, 1963, Ch. 1; W. G. Moulton, *A Linguistic Guide to Language Learning*, 2nd ed., Modern Language Association of America, 1970, Ch. 3 'How language works'; D. Crystal, *Introduction to Linguistic Pathology*, London, Arnold, 1980, Ch. 3 'The communication chain'.

the sperm to produce the foetus or the overheated blood of menstruation. If words can accomplish things, this is not by reason of having any 'performative' function. Words are themselves things in a domain of things.[7]

The first point I wish to make about the comparison is that if it is true that one cannot fathom the D-account without placing it in the context of Dogon culture and its traditional preoccupations, the same applies equally to the E-account with regard to Western culture. In that respect, they are on an absolutely equal footing.

The second point I wish to make is this. From the perspective of someone who accepts the E-account, it seems reasonable to say that the D-account is, as a whole, both inadequate and misleading. But it would be no less reasonable to say that, from the perspective of someone who accepts the D-account, the E-account is too. These judgements would be not so much comments on particular terms or distinctions as upon the total picture underlying them. For that is what relates the particular terms and distinctions to one another, thus rendering discourse couched in the metalanguage internally coherent.

It is this totality that I am referring to when I speak of *metalinguistic frameworks*. The notion is useful, if only because a description of a metalinguistic framework allows us to locate certain problems. For instance, it is clear that the debate considered in Chapter 8 between Ayer and his critics bears on a particular feature in the metalinguistic framework provided by the E-account. It is about what goes on in that crucial initial phase

---

[7] S. Auroux, *La Révolution technique de la grammatisation*, Liège, Mardaga, 1994, p. 38.

concerning the formulation of a message inside the head of the speaker. Ayer is contesting the traditional view that there is an independent non-verbal phase of the formulation. But he is not contesting any *other* feature of the 'speech circuit' picture – the activation of the organs of speech, the transmission of sound waves, etc. He addresses only speech production, as distinct from reception, and only one phase of that.

Similarly, one could imagine that a maverick D-account theorist might contest the received wisdom as to whether the right lung is filled before the left in the production of good speech. In challenging the accepted view, the iconoclast might well encounter terminological difficulties if the traditional D-metalanguage already *identifies* good speech as that produced by filling the right lung first. The point is that such challenges only make sense *within* the metalinguistic framework provided. They do not attack the framework as such, but seek to modify some detail of it.

Now it might be urged that there is much in common between the D-account and the E-account. (This itself might even be held to be of some significance, since little was known in Europe about Dogon metalanguage until quite recently, and it is historically unlikely that the Dogon had ever been influenced by acquaintance with European views of language.) Among the common features are the following: (i) that speech is envisaged as involving an interaction between two individuals (*A* and *B*); (ii) that it is initiated by one individual (*A*) and affects the other (*B*); (iii) that speech involves transmission through air waves; (iv) that the organs of transmission include *A*'s mouth; and (v) the process of reception goes via *B*'s ears.

To anyone who wishes to say that this concordance between two metalinguistic frameworks is entirely unremarkable because it merely recognizes what is obvious, my immediate response has to be to question why these features in particular should be recognized as 'obvious' – as opposed to the remaining features of the two frameworks, which are far from being so. But there is a more subtle point here too. Even my *identification* of five 'common features' presupposes a comparative procedure which implicitly validates the Western approach to analysing such an account. It does not allow for any competing analysis that a Dogon perspective might suggest. Thus if a Dogon theorist failed to see anything in common at all between the two accounts, or if, on the contrary, the Dogon theorist saw no difference whatever except in terminology, these analyses would simply have to be rejected by a Western colleague. In short, comparability here means Western comparability, *which is itself based on taking a certain view of how language relates to the world outside language.*

It cannot be said that the D-account is, on the whole, any more 'mythical' than the E-account. To be sure, a supporter of the E-account might well object that no one has ever isolated the hypothesized verbal fluid or observed the spiral rotation that feature in the D-account. But that merely reflects a preference for certain sorts of 'evidence'. Furthermore, a supporter of the D-account might well counterattack, if such a debate were engaged, by pointing out that no one has ever seen an atomic concept in the human brain, of the kind which features in the E-account. And if the process by which the direction of spiral rotation of verbal vapour determines the beneficial or noxious properties of the liquid which the hearer swallows seems somewhat mysterious, it can hardly be more mysterious than the way in which speaker and hearer in the E-account are provided with matching stored sets of concepts and sound patterns. Finally, although a supporter of the E-account might protest that the D-account simply omits the cognitive phase of 'understanding' altogether, a D-account supporter might complain in return that the E-account does not explain how speech can cause bodily effects, such as tears, laughter, blushing, etc.

In short, it would be pretentious of me to claim that anything in my own linguistic experience leads me immediately to reject the D-account and embrace the E-account. As it happens, some features of both accounts seem to me highly questionable. But this is not intended as a plea for metalinguistic relativism (if that is inter-preted as claiming that any metalanguage is as good as any other). What I do know – at least – is something about the development of and the particular cultural needs that are served by the E-account, whereas I would be out of my depth in discussing comparable matters in relation to the D-account.

All this comes down to in the end is that my education was a Western education and the Western metalinguistic tradition is fairly well 'documented' (another key Western term). Corresponding answers in the Dogon case would be far more 'speculative' (from a Western point of view), because there is no corresponding 'history' of Dogon metalanguage.

What I find somewhat paradoxical is that it is in the well 'documented' history that one finds an almost total imperviousness to historicity. Western philosophers and linguists alike – from Plato down to Wittgenstein and from the *modistae* down to Saussure – regard themselves as dealing with 'timeless' questions about language that are somehow intrinsic to the subject.

Although it is recognized that there are languages in some parts of the world in which it would be impossible to formulate all the metalinguistic questions which Europeans ask, and although it is conceded that even in languages as closely related to one another as English, French, German and Greek the metalinguistic terminology is not exactly equivalent, nevertheless in practice these considerations have never deterred Western scholars from proceeding as if their own metalinguistic questions had a universal validity. Furthermore, European linguists have invariably described non-European languages on the basis of models drawn from European grammar. It is as if the employment of a particular metalanguage somehow licensed its users to ask the basic questions about language on behalf of all humanity.

This seems to me the biggest metalinguistic mistake of all. For as soon as we begin to examine the relevant history in any detail, what becomes abundantly clear is that Western metalanguage, far from offering a sound basis for universal linguistic inquiry, is actually geared in the first instance to very parochial linguistic concerns. These arise from the programmes and aims of a certain (Western) form of education, and it is here that we must look if we wish to understand *why* the metalanguage has most of the features it has.

Chapter 10
METALINGUISTIC ILLUSIONS

One general objection may by now have occurred to the reader of the preceding chapters. Although the author has displayed considerable scepticism about the metalanguage in which linguistic inquiry has been conducted in the Western tradition, and in particular about certain metalinguistic 'doctrines', as he calls them, nevertheless his own discussion of these matters has been couched in precisely the kind of terminology he regards as suspect. In practice, he seems to accept, in common with those supposedly benighted philosophers and grammarians whom he criticizes, that we can – and must – distinguish between words and their use, between sentences and what they mean, etc. He even seems to concede that there are recognizably recurrent linguistic forms and combinations of forms. So does he not, in the end, defeat his own critical strategy by the very way he argues his case?

The above criticism might be pressed even harder. How, it might be asked, can *anyone* deny the legitimacy of such distinctions without necessarily falling into this trap? For to deny that, for instance, *The cat sat on the mat* contains two examples of the definite article or three of the letter *a* is already to acknowledge metalinguistically those very units ('the definite article', 'the letter *a*') the sceptic rejects. Thus the denial is self-defeating. All the sceptic has succeeded in doing is hoisting himself with his own petard.

147

Any reader inclined to entertain objections along these lines must, I think, have mistaken the theoretical thrust and purpose of my argument. The intention was never to call a halt to the metalinguistic games we play when we inquire into language, but to prevent the fact that we play them as we do from giving rise to metalinguistic illusions. That, unfortunately, all too frequently happens.

Let us go back to the two doctrines that came under attack in Chapter 1. Both are based on the theoretical misconstrual of certain common lay practices. These practices include oral repetition, quotation, reporting speech *verbatim* (as it is revealingly called), copying documents and recital of memorized texts. (There are others, but the ones I have just listed will do for my present purposes.) Now at first sight this claim might seem to be tantamount to putting one's head in the lion's mouth. For do not all these practices involve, precisely, the iteration of words, sentences, etc.? And is not this feature of deliberate verbal iteration exactly what sets these practices apart from 'ordinary' speech and writing?

My reply is that the rhetorical force of these questions derives from an uncritical acceptance of exactly the doctrines that I am objecting to. The issue is not whether or how we recognize the difference between cases of iteration and non-iteration in language: the issue concerns the interpretation of that difference. What I am claiming is that the doctrines I reject supply a highly questionable interpretation, and are responsible for the academic perpetuation of a metalinguistic muddle.

Sorting out the muddle does not require anything as ambitious as the construction of a new error-free metalanguage (a project about which I am sceptical, as is evident from Chapter 8). But it does require us to recognize that the reflexivity of language cannot be contained in the ways these doctrines implicitly claim.

In the preceding chapters I have tried to show how the doctrine of use and mention and the doctrine of types and tokens interlock with five other doctrines to support a 'segregational' view of language. The other five doctrines were:

(i) the doctrine of parts of speech,
(ii) the doctrine of sentences and propositions,
(iii) the doctrine of telementation,
(iv) the doctrine of fixed codes, and
(v) the doctrine of plain representation.

Why 'doctrines'? I call all seven 'doctrines' because, at one time or another, they have actually been *taught* (by philosophers, linguists and others) in schools and universities. But I think all seven have humbler origins. These doctrines arise from everyday lay discourse about language. They are misguided attempts to provide general answers to questions which never called for general answers in the first place.

Take *'What is that called?'*, which I have already touched upon in Chapter 7. In everyday circumstances, anyone who asks this question as a genuine request for information hopes that the addressee will be able to supply an appropriate word or words for 'that' (i.e. for whatever is indicated, whether verbally or non-verbally, either by the questioner or by some other participant, in the communication situation in question). 'That' may be something the questioner points to, describes, does, touches, sees taking place, etc.

The trouble begins when a theorist takes this question as an invitation to construct a general explanation covering *every* 'that' and *every* verbal item that might feature as the interlocutor's response. Or, if not *every* one, a fairly representative selection. In other words, what happens is that the theorist treats the lay question as an intellectual challenge. This challenge is dealt with by extrapolating from the original question to a higher-order metalinguistic question of the form: 'What is it for *x* to be called *X*?'. This move, I am saying, is a mistake, and the supposedly higher-order question is a nonsense. There just isn't anything 'that it is' for *x* to be called *X*.

How does this absurd mistake come about? Why do so many theorists make it? My answer is that it is a very easy mistake to make for anyone operating within the Western metalinguistic framework. It comes about because a feature of the original question-and-answer format has been treated as reflecting the underlying structure of relationships between words and things. Samuel Johnson once observed that 'words are the daughters of earth and things are the sons of heaven'. If we make due allowance for Johnson's religious convictions and the metaphor, it would be difficult to epitomize more accurately the conception which the Western metalinguistic framework projects. (The 'due allowance', of course, may be contested; but I shall not stop to contest it here.) My point is that *because* the sibling relationship can apparently be established, i.e. *because* – at least, in so many cases – a simple answer *can* be given (Q. 'What is that flower called?' A. 'It is called a *geranium*.'), the assumption is made that matching up every 'that' with 'what it is called' is a task of the same order as matching up two objects given in advance. (Cf. Q. 'Where is the key to this lock?' A. 'Here it is.' Q. 'Which is your car, sir?' A. 'It's the one over there parked next to the Fiat.' Keys and locks, cars and their drivers, are all neatly paired up – or assumed to be – before the question is ever asked.)

The model of already-matching pairs is transposed to the metalinguistic case for no better reason than that the question-and-answer format is roughly similar.

Now this, if I am right, is a howler of the most elementary kind. But it is disguised by the way our Western metalinguistic framework is structured. In short, it is simple-minded in the extreme to extrapolate from (i) the pairing relationship that features in the lay format to (ii) the assumption that the way 'words' relate to 'things' actually *is* an example of such a relationship. But the howler is not immediately apparent because it does not jar with the metalinguistic formulations that are current – or traditional – in our discussions of the question. When we tell someone – quite rightly – that this flower is called a *geranium* we are supplying exactly the answer that was needed. But it does not follow from this success that language works by furnishing verbal labels for all the things provided in advance by God, Nature or some other agency.

The mistake is on a par with supposing that because a sensible answer can usually be given to the question 'How much does this cost?' (A. 'It costs £10.') it follows that an economic system basically comprises a set of binary correlations between prices and what can be bought. Anyone who made this kind of mistake would never survive a first-year course in economics. But in linguistics and philosophy no less fundamental errors have paraded for centuries as orthodox wisdom.

* * *

Just to show that '*What is that called?*' is not an exceptional case, let us now consider for purposes of comparison '*What does that mean?*'.

If I ask this (as a genuine request for information

about an unknown or problematic word or words), I am asking the addressee to supply an alternative word or words (to fit the occasion). E.g. Q. 'What does *noxious* mean?' A. 'It means *harmful*.' Q. 'What does *confiture* mean?' A. 'It means *jam*.'

Here again the theorist leaps in to ask a higher-order question, or even a whole series of them. Thus, for example, we find Strawson opening a paper on 'Meaning, truth and communication' by firing off the following interrogative barrage.

> What is it for anything to have a *meaning* at all, in the way, or in the sense, in which words or sentences or signals have meaning? What is it for a particular sentence to have the meaning or meanings that it does have? What is it for a particular phrase, or a particular word, to have the meaning or meanings it does have?[1]

Here is an eminent philosopher opting for an all-out frontal assault on the metalinguistic fortress. The possibility does not seem to be entertained that maybe the opening salvoes are entirely misdirected, that maybe there *isn't* any 'what' that 'it is' for 'anything to have a meaning at all', etc. So where do these front-line questions come from? Again, it seems to me, they are concocted by extrapolating from the quite ordinary and sensible question 'What does that mean?' (as posed by the lay inquirer seeking lay information). *Why* are they concocted? Because their concoction sets the theorist up in the business of linguistic inquiry and lays out the limits within which the intellectual search will be conducted.

---

[1]   P. F. Strawson, 'Meaning, truth and communication', in N. Minnis (ed.), *Linguistics at Large*, St. Albans, Paladin, 1973, p. 91.

The result is exactly as in the case of '*What is that called?*'. It is all too readily assumed that there will be *something* (concrete or abstract, physical or psychological) that can be produced as the semantic partner to the verbal item(s) in question.

Again, the pairing which is a feature of the lay question-and-answer format is misconstrued not only as reflecting the 'real' relationship between linguistic forms and linguistic meanings but also as providing a blueprint for the form that any general semantic inquiry must take.

In both cases the fact that the original format involves juxtaposing pairs of items (*x* versus *X*, or *X* versus *Y*) is implicitly taken as calling for a theory which spells out a general relationship between *x* and *X*, or *X* and *Y*. Binary pairings become not just the order of the day, or the flavour of the month, but the exemplar of the connection which *must* obtain in order to allow such questions to be asked and such answers given.

Here linguistic theory achieves the illusion of self-levitation by the simple expedient of tugging insistently at its own metalinguistic shoelaces.

* * *

If there are any readers for whom the above arguments are too 'meta' altogether, let me try a more direct approach.

According to the standard doctrine of use and mention, what I am supposed to be doing when I tell you that Peter said 'John has pneumonia' is giving you the name of the sentence Peter uttered. But it seems highly unlikely that I am doing anything of the kind. For one thing, as it happens, I do not know what the name of that sentence is, or even whether it has one. In my linguistic experience – which is admittedly limited, but the only experience I can go by – people, towns, mountains, dogs, hurricanes and many other things often have names; but not sentences. Nor does it seem any more plausible to say that what I did was give you not the name but a *description* of Peter's sentence. I did neither of these things. All I did, to the best of my knowledge, was *repeat* what Peter said. But I no more need to know the name of a sentence in order to repeat it than I need to know the name of the tune Peter was whistling in order to repeat that. Nor is my repetition, either in the verbal or the musical example, a description, a designation, or anything of the kind. No names, descriptions, designations, etc. are involved, and to claim otherwise is metalinguistic gobbledegook.

Anyone can see that there is *something* fishy about the doctrine of use and mention by considering such a simple institutionalized practice as a roll-call. (The procedure will be familiar to anyone who has taken part in it. Roughly, John Smith is expected to say 'Yes', or 'Present', or 'Aye aye, sir', or stand up, or salute, or otherwise indicate his presence, when the teacher, sergeant, or whoever else is in charge calls out 'John Smith'.) It is clear that the use-or-mention theorist is here in a trilemma. Three theoretical possibilities arise. (i) Calling out 'John Smith' is a conventional substitute for the question 'Is John Smith here?'. (ii) Calling out 'John Smith' is a conventional substitute for the question 'Is there anyone here by the name of "John Smith"?'. (iii) Calling out 'John Smith' is ambiguous as between (i) and (ii).

We should note that it is not expected that anyone should respond: (iv) 'Yes, I am here; but my name is not "John Smith".' Once the inadmissibility of (iv) in this particular (meta)language-game is recognized, we should – I suggest – see where the the doctrine of use and mention gets it wrong. The doctrine decontextualizes the whole procedure.

If any readers doubt this, let them pursue the question of what is meant if John Smith answers 'Yes', or 'Aye aye, sir', or whatever. (Here the distinction between a verbal and a non-verbal response is immaterial, provided it is recognized as a response.) It may be, for instance, that the individual in question has various aliases. To some, he is known as 'John Smith'. To others, he is known as 'Santa Claus'. But then, to others the person called 'Santa Claus' may be the well-known politician whose name 'in real life' is 'John Major' or 'Jacques Chirac'. At this point we lose track of the nomenclatural inverted commas. (Quite understandably: they were invented by MI5 or whatever other agency wished its records to distinguish between, or conflate, those on the pay-roll and those on the hit list. There is no actuarial contradiction between employing and killing an individual. It may even balance the books.)

But the mere fact that it offers three different interpretations of names in roll-call procedures or records argues strongly against the doctrine of use and mention. Nor is this an 'exception'. An analogous case is voting in an election. Do you, by placing your cross in a certain 'box' on the ballot slip, affirm something about a candidate, or about your preferred candidate's name, or about both? If ever an elector had seriously been bothered by such problems, there would at least be a *prima facie* case for pursuing them theoretically.

To see that these are rubbish questions is to grasp something more about the linguistic role of names than the doctrine of use and mention admits. No one will get very far by turning up at the polling booth next day claiming that there was a misunderstanding. (This has not dismayed – and may even have encouraged – unscrupulous would-be politicians who change their names legally in order to mislead gullible voters. The point is that the electoral procedure (in the U.K.) – quite rightly – puts the onus on the voters to find out which candidates go by which names, for electoral purposes. It does not *in addition* require voters to find out what the names of the names are. But it does require them to recognize the written form of the names.)

But there are more serious theoretical reasons for doubting the doctrine of use and mention. If ""John"" is the name of "John", then such names-of-names constitute a bizarre exception to the arbitrariness of the linguistic sign. For in order to recognize it as such (i.e. as *n*-of-*n*) it is either necessary (i) to know the form of the original name (i.e. *n*), or else (ii) to realize that the form of *n*-of-*n* (setting aside any added inverted commas, or similar first-aid devices recommended by proponents of the doctrine) is systematically ambiguous at an indefinite number of recursive levels. In other words, a unique kind of linguistic 'rule' must apply to cases of *n*-of-*n*; namely, that mere acquaintance with such a designation automatically informs one about what it designates. Now this is odd, because no other kind of linguistic sign behaves in a similar way. If it did, then there would be no need for language-learning. (From the form *confiture* it would already be clear to everybody that jam is what is designated.) This consideration *in itself* is sufficient to throw serious doubt upon the *n*-of-*n* analysis.

It is at this juncture that the doctrine of types and tokens comes to the rescue of the doctrine of use and mention. In effect, what is proposed is that there is no problem here, because language operates under a universal dispensation by which *all* linguistic tokens *manifest* (in Peirce's terminology 'are signs of') their linguistic types. So anyone who has not understood this has not understood something very fundamental about how language works. All that needs to be understood in addition is that, for reasons of convenience and economy, everyday speech allows every token to function as a sign of at least two types. Thus the token *John* can occur as a sign of two types, one standing for the person and the other standing for his name.

But this explanation, patently, is either sheer magic or else metaphysical obfuscation. Nothing else in the universe works like this. So why should it work for words? Mere inspection of an object does not tell you what kind of thing it is, what it 'stands for', or where exactly in fits into the Great Scheme of Things (if there is one).

What, then, you ask again, is the *fons et origo* of these misguided doctrines? The answer seems to me obvious enough. They arise from a misconstrual of lay metalinguistic discourse, coupled to an educational *fait accompli*. For their own professional purposes, philosophers who have not yet abandoned the proposition altogether are still (however reluctantly) committed to trying to force all assertions into that ancient mould, while linguists are equally – albeit more enthusiastically – committed to squeezing any utterance whatsoever into the Procrustean bed of the sentence.

The only kind of analysis available within these reductive programmes requires propositions and sentences to have subjects, subjects to be realized in speech or writing by names, noun phrases, etc. Therefore, somehow or other, in cases of verbatim report, quotation, etc., the verbal expression of the reported or quoted item must willy-nilly be construed as a 'name', 'designation', or something similar. For otherwise the utterance defies analysis altogether.

In short, an everyday metalinguistic practice like verbatim repetition is here being treated as if it were exactly analogous to reporting any non-linguistic event. What this fails to allow for is the complexity of contextualization which makes repetition what it is. Repetition requires that an utterance be integrated into a series of activities, both verbal and non-verbal, according to a certain pattern. This integration is what gives repetition its meaning. Thus *Peter said 'John has pneumonia'*, if it is a genuine case of verbatim repetition, is linguistically quite unlike the report *Peter baked a cake*. Both tell us what Peter did. But in the latter case there is nothing which corresponds to the matching requirements which govern, in the former case, the form of words in the report. If we do not grasp those requirements then we do not even begin to understand what linguistic reflexivity involves.

The doctrine of use and mention simply misrepresents linguistic reflexivity in these cases by trying to construe it in terms of a model that works for reports in general. It extrapolates from the supposedly unproblematic case of *Peter baked a cake* to *Peter said 'John has pneumonia'*. The extrapolation is based on using metalinguistic terms like 'name' to gloss over the awkward disparity between the linguistic procedures involved. The extrapolation, moreover, is bought at a rather cheap price from the philosopher's point of view, i.e. a proliferation in the use of inverted commas and a potentially infinite multiplication of linguistic items. Thus any form (e.g. *John*) will itself have a name (*"John"*), which in turn will have a name (*""John""*), and so on ad infinitum. These extensions, it should be noted, are 'logically' necessary as far as the philosopher is concerned. For although in everyday affairs we may not have many occasions to talk about the names of names of names, nevertheless what will be true of them will not be true of *their* names. And this, it will be recalled, was the original motivation for distinguishing between *suppositio formalis* and *suppositio materialis*. In short, the doctrine of use and mention is a licence for philosophers and linguists to print their own money.

Let us now turn again to the doctrine of types and tokens, which is another such licence. According to this, what I was doing when I told you what Peter said (i.e. 'John has pneumonia') was producing new linguistic tokens of exactly the same types of which Peter previously produced tokens in the original utterance. But I find this theoretical account of my action entirely unconvincing too: in the first place, because I have no idea what 'linguistic types' – if any – lay behind the original utterance. In other words, if I had had to achieve that linguistic objective which the doctrine of types and tokens sets for me in my attempt to tell you what Peter said, I would have had no idea of how to set about it. But I do, in fact, know what I was doing; and it wasn't that at all. I was simply recounting an episode of my *own* linguistic experience, i.e. telling you what I understood Peter as saying when I heard him speak.

Thus the doctrine of types and tokens also misrepresents linguistic reflexivity. For it allows no place for an essential feature of verbatim repetition, i.e. that it involves self-report. Furthermore, insisting on the production of tokens of the original types in order to present an 'accurate' or 'correct' report is to set a target which is logically – and not merely psychologically – impossible of fulfilment. For the type-token relation may be set up in all kinds of ways. (Even if we set aside Peirce's controversial claim that each token is a *sign* of its type. This leads straight into a labyrinth of problems about signs, which I cannot enter here.) The trouble with the doctrine of types and tokens is that it is too flexible rather than too rigid. It does not tell us, in short, what the type-token ratio is supposed to be for. Peirce's paradigm example was counting the number of words on a page. But even here there may be other purposes than the printer's concern with the length of the text. Does it matter, for instance, whether capital letters occur? Are *The* and *the* tokens of the same type, or tokens of two different types? Is there just one type underlying the definite article in spoken English? Or does it depend on how the vowel is pronounced? Do the first three letters of *theatre* also count as a *the*-token? The doctrine itself offers no clear answers to such questions. Nor could it. For the abstractions Peirce calls 'types' are no more than a function of the interest we take in certain counting procedures and certain similarities. (If they *are* more than that, then we are back in the murky metaphysical underworld of Plato's Forms.)

What ultimately condemns the doctrine of types and tokens is that its arguments patently misconstrue its own metalinguistic proposals. (It is rather like a bad advertising campaign, which unwittingly exposes the defects of the product it is supposed to promote.) For there is no doubt that it is possible to set up metalinguistically a variety of conflicting type-token analyses for any collection of texts or corpus of utterances. The idea that in any given case there will be just one such analysis which 'really' reflects the structure of 'the language' used is a metalinguistic illusion.

This is typical of the process by which metalinguistic illusions are conjured up. A lay metalinguistic practice is reinterpreted in terms which imply that it is actually something quite different. This reinterpretation is then fed back into the semantics of the lay terms themselves: e.g. *repetition* comes to be defined ('technically' or 'scientifically') as the production of tokens of the same type. What we have here is academic self-deception of the same ilk as supposing that the lay concept 'two' can be given a mathematically exact explication as 'the class of pair-classes'.

The problem for many university students today, both in philosophy and in linguistics, is that they are introduced to the approved technical metalanguage before they have any clear idea of why or how it comes to be available, or what issues its availability either promotes or obscures. They are then expected to write essays which deploy this academic jargon, in order to demonstrate to their teachers that they have mastered it. In other words, once they are in the academic fairground and installed on the metalinguistic merry-go-round, it is not in their power to stop it or ask to get off.

Unfortunately, to 'give the right answer' when asked 'How many words are there in *Fish swim* ?', or 'What is the predicate in *Socrates is mortal* ?', or 'How many *a*'s are there in *anabaptist* ?' is not an indication that the student – or anyone else – has at last grasped the fundamental mechanisms of language. (Any more than giving the right answer to the question 'What class is designated by the term *two*?' shows that the student has at last understood arithmetic.) All the students have grasped is how to play a certain kind of metalinguistic game. That may be sufficient for their immediate purposes, and they may get high marks in class for playing it: but whether getting high marks in class leads to any clearer understanding of language is another question.

The general advice one might give to those who would like to get off this particular merry-go-round is to bear in mind, when assessing what philosophers and linguists say about language, that there is no reason at all to regard iteration that involves speech or writing as any different in principle from other kinds of iteration. A knock at the door may be repeated. But the second knock supplies neither the name nor the description of the first. Nor does it make much sense to insist that unless the second knock were actually a token of the same type as the first we should not recognize it as a case of repetition. For that would be to beg the question of what degree of similarity must obtain between tokens of a single type, as well as misidentifying a terminological problem as a psychological one.

The sources of most of the metalinguistic illusions that have flourished in the Western tradition are faults in the basic metalinguistic framework. The central fault is to treat linguistic reflexivity as parasitic upon a more basic non-reflexive function of language, something extra to the primary purposes words serve. These primary purposes, allegedly, have to do with the world that lies beyond language and exists independently of it. They involve what I called in an earlier chapter the 'pragmatic network'. Thus it is assumed that the primary function of a linguistic form like *John* is to identify a particular individual, and the fact that this form also identifies that individual's name (as in answer to the question 'What is your name?') is seen as a kind of unexpected bonus. Reflexivity is thus marginalized and indeed only accommodated at all by the expedient of treating the name itself as a separate, independently existing object, like the individual so named. Thus arises the view of names as vocal labels, the view of meaning as a relation in which one thing 'stands for' another, and, by extension, the view of languages as nomenclatures. All three have featured prominently in segregational theorizing about language in the Western tradition.[2]

The error in the two doctrines discussed in the present chapter is that both try to treat linguistic reflexivity as a feature of our verbal equipment rather than as a feature of the communication process. Intellectually, the mistake is on a par with believing that the value of a ten-dollar bill resides in the actual piece of paper, not in the economic process it is part of.

Linguistic reflexivity is a far more pervasive feature of verbal communication than can be accounted for by postulating a special class of expressions (i.e. *names* of words, of sentences, etc.) endowed with the unlikely property of being isomorphic with what they designate. Linguistic reflexivity derives from our whole engagement in language as communicators. It is inherent in the game, not just in a few of the verbal counters with which the game is played. And unless we grasped that, we could no more be participating members of any linguistic community than we could play chess without understanding our role as players.

It is interesting to ask why spoken languages do not have oral devices corresponding to those inverted commas so favoured by proponents of the doctrine of use and mention. In other words, why do spoken languages fail to distinguish phonetically in some systematic way between 'John' as a reply to 'Who is that?' and 'John' as a reply to 'What is his name?'? The reason is quite simple. Linguistically, we are not dealing with two different items here but with a single item. To insist that there must be two because of the ambiguity of saying *John is monosyllabic* is rather like insisting

---

[2]   For discussion, see R. Harris, *The Language-Makers*, London, Duckworth, 1980.

that there must be two homophonous words for oil because *Oil is rising* might be a comment either on the latest drilling or on the latest prices. We no more need two ways of saying *John* than we need two ways of saying *oil*. If there is any risk of confusion, we can always be more precise (*The name John is monosyllabic*, *The price of oil is rising*, etc.). But the possibility of greater precision is no proof that there were two homophonous linguistic units in the first place.

In order to grasp what a name is (or any other kind of word for that matter) we have to grasp a certain pattern of relationships that includes our own role – as speakers and hearers, writers and readers – in the communicational process. Any theory which does not acknowledge this oversimplifies our linguistic experience in the crudest possible way. Recognition of the reflexivity of language is not marginal but central to linguistic communication. To know one's own name – which most of us know at a very early age – is already to recognize that reflexivity, and to recognize it is also to grasp the communicational concept of self. It involves realizing that you, your name and various other words like *I* and *me* are integrated into a communicational programme that is different from anyone else's. It is on this basis – and no other – that we enter into membership of a linguistic community. Our role in that community is not reducible to functioning as anonymous, interchangeable speakers and hearers. If it were, then language would be forever beyond our comprehension (as well as leading to intolerable confusion in the conduct of our daily affairs).

To see this is to see why language has always eluded the comprehension of Western grammarians and logicians. For in their schematizations, the individual *qua* individual does not have to be anything other than the possible bearer of a name, the possible referent of a referring expression, and a possible speaker or hearer. Thus the notion of speech as a creative, interactive function of individuals is replaced by the notion of speech as a machinery producing a series of autonomous verbal objects. These objects are all treated as replicas of independently existing patterns. Once the relevant patterns are identified, the replicas can then be analysed with respect to their internal structure, by analytic techniques that the grammarian and the logician have developed for just such a purpose. In short, speech ceases to be treated as speech and is subjected to a decontextualizing process. Speech goes in at one end and sentences, propositions and other metalinguistic abstractions come out at the other.

To understand the inevitable contortions and compressions involved in the operation of this metalinguistic sausage-machine (and the long-standing professional agendas it serves) does not take us as far along the road as we might like towards an adequate theory of language. But at least it is a first step in the right direction.

POSTSCRIPT

Post-war philosophy, according to Strawson, relied mainly on two very divergent techniques for dealing with linguistic problems.[1] One technique (pioneered by Carnap) involved the construction of artificial languages, whose properties were carefully selected and regimented. The advantage of this technique, it was claimed, is to reveal more clearly structures and relations which may be obscured by 'the looseness, the untidiness, the shifting complexities of common speech'. The other technique, which was quite opposite in orientation, involved paying minute attention to the details of everyday usage. This technique (championed by Austin) claimed the advantage of refusing to oversimplify the complicated ways in which human beings actually speak and reason. Philosophy, on this view, simply could not afford to oversimplify. 'For it is the most general, most fundamental and most ordinary ideas which give rise to the major problems of philosophy.'

However, by the 1970s neither the 'artificial language' programme nor the 'ordinary language' programme was doing too well. And a serious competitor had appeared on the scene.

---

[1] The quotations in this paragraph are from P. F. Strawson, 'Construction and analysis', in A. J. Ayer *et al.*, *The Revolution in Philosophy*, London, Macmillan, 1956, pp. 97–110.

The philosopher who in 1971 edited a volume entitled *Philosophy and Linguistics* referred in his Introduction to the current 'problem of working out a *modus vivendi* with linguistics'.[2] The problem, as he saw it, arose from the recent development of generative grammar, and the ensuing claim that 'the linguistic scientist is now equipped to do with proper professionalism what the philosopher has in the past done in a more amateurish and piecemeal way'. Hence the perception that 'linguistics as a subject appears [...] to compete with philosophy as a subject'.

The general editor of the series in which that volume appeared voiced similar concerns:

> If it is once granted that philosophy is a conceptual inquiry, and hence concerned in some way with the uses of words, then the question arises of what are its proper relations with linguistic science. If they are competitors, then does not this put the philosopher in the uneasy position of the witch-doctor confronted by the scientifically qualified medico, the untrained manager up against the graduate of the Harvard Business School?[3]

Whether that perception of interdisciplinary competition still persists, or whether the rise of 'cognitive science' in the meantime has somehow resolved the problem, are not questions that it is proposed to pursue here. This book, as I have already said, is not a survey of contemporary relations between philosophy and linguistics, nor of the history of relations between those disciplines or their predecessors in earlier periods.

---

[2] C. Lyas (ed.), *Philosophy and Linguistics*, London, Macmillan, 1971, p. 12.

[3] A. G. N. Flew, in *Philosophy and Linguistics*, p. 6.

Nevertheless, it is interesting to note that in the early 1970s philosophers were talking of 'competition' from linguistics. There was no mention of 'competition' from nuclear physics or biochemistry or any other subject. This in itself is a measure of the extent to which philosophers had come to identify philosophy as depending in some way on the investigation of language as one of its central concerns.

Furthermore, although philosophers could claim for their interest in language a respectable ancestry, going back as far as the pre-Socratics, nevertheless to broach the subject of reaching a *modus vivendi* between philosophy and linguistics sounded a new note. It was, at least to a linguist's ear, a quite different tune from the one which philosophers had been singing earlier in the century. Then there had been no question of even seeking the opinion of linguists on linguistic matters, much less fearing competition.

Wittgenstein's *Tractatus Logico-Philosophicus* had proclaimed the controversial doctrine that 'all philosophy is a critique of language'. Wittgenstein adds cryptically, 'though not in Mauthner's sense'. The reference is to Mauthner's *Beiträge zu einer Kritik der Sprache* (1901–2). Although Mauthner is often regarded as the first of the 'linguistic philosophers', and introduced in advance of Wittgenstein the notion of a *Spielregel*, it is arguable that the palm should be awarded to Alexander Bryan Johnson, whose *Treatise on Language* was published in 1836. For in this work Johnson developed the Baconian theme which was to be echoed by many later philosophers; namely, the necessity of studying language in order to root out intellectual errors promoted by the 'verbal defects...inseparable from language'.

In his Introduction to Wittgenstein's *Tractatus*, Bertrand Russell wrote:

> There are various problems as regards language. First, there is the problem of what actually occurs in our minds when we use language with the intention of meaning something by it: this problem belongs to psychology. Secondly, there is the problem as to what is the relation subsisting between thoughts, words or sentences, and that which they refer to or mean; this problem belongs to epistemology. Thirdly, there is the problem of using sentences so as to convey truth rather than falsehood; this belongs to the special sciences dealing with the subject-matter in question. Fourthly, there is the question: what relation must one fact (such as a sentence) have to another in order to be *capable* of being a symbol for that other? This last is a logical question, and is the one with which Mr. Wittgenstein is concerned.[4]

What must have puzzled any linguist who read this pronouncement was the absence from Russell's list of any *linguistic* problem (i.e. one which a student of linguistics would have recognized as falling within the domain of expertise of the linguist). One possibility, obviously, was that a Cambridge philosopher in 1920 simply did not *recognize* any such problem. It is indeed rare to find in the writings of any philosopher of the interwar period even a mention of the work of any leading linguistic theorist, much less a detailed discussion of the concepts employed in linguistics. (This alone gives the lie to the oft-repeated claim that

---

[4] P. ix of the 1961 rev. edition of the *Tractatus*, London, Routledge & Kegan Paul.

philosophy holds some kind of general watching brief over intellectual progress and concepts developed in other subjects. For here was a subject in which philosophers had lately declared a vital interest, but shown no inclination at all to find out what was actually going on in the relevant academic area.)

From a linguist's point of view, therefore, there was inevitably something dubious about what was retrospectively called the great 'linguistic turn' (whatever that curious phrase might be taken to mean) in twentieth-century philosophy. It was rather as if one's neighbour had suddenly declared a serious interest in gardening; but on looking over the fence one saw that what this amounted to was that the neighbour had mown a small area of grass in the midst of his wilderness, on which to pitch his deckchair in summer.

Linguists of a more sceptical turn of mind doubtless viewed philosophy's new agenda as just another stage in the long retreat from the commanding academic position once held by philosophers in times gone by. In this perspective, twentieth-century philosophy seems to be something left over from a long vanished intellectual scene in which the philosopher occupied centre stage and was expected to be an authority on many different things. These included all human behaviour, society, art, morality and the physical universe in its entirety. The first Western philosopher to tackle this formidable range of inquiry in a more or less systematic way was Aristotle. The last was probably Diderot. What eventually strangled philosophy as practised in the intervening centuries was the vast increase of empirical specialization that began to accumulate in Europe from the Renaissance onwards. In one sense, philosophy *qua* general inquiry into whatever-there-was-to-be-known was defeated by its own success. Knowledge expanded until there was too much to know and too many experts on little fragments of it.

It was not simply a question of reaching a point where too much new information was available for any *one* philosopher to handle. What killed off 'encyclopedic' philosophy was not, ultimately, that the lifespan of the average human being proved to be far too short to acquire expertise in so many different fields. Philosophy had succumbed, rather, to a linguistic virus. The expansion of knowledge fostered an unprecedented verbal diversification. In the new domains of empirical expertise, no common language was spoken. Each specialized field of knowledge developed its own. Whereas the language of Aristotle's *Physics* is roughly the same as the language of his *Politics*, one has only to open a modern encyclopedia and read the articles on, say, economics and jurisprudence to realize that it is no longer possible to follow what experts say in such diverse fields without specific linguistic guidance. Insofar as modern philosophers engage in the philosophy of economics, law, physics, etc., they are themselves obliged to learn the language of those specialized fields.

The explosion of language and the resulting communication problem contributed significantly to rendering the position of the philosopher as universal *savant* untenable. The philosopher had lost the linguistic initiative in the formulation and discussion of issues. It was also in part what dictated the academic strategy for the modern retrenchment of philosophy. (Philosophers may prefer to speak of a 'redefinition' of their subject, rather than 'retrenchment'; but if the necessity for redefinition is dictated by forces beyond one's control, it begins to look suspiciously like retrenchment to most people.)

The lengthy historical retreat from the Western faith in the philosopher as polymath went through various phases which – from a non-philosopher's point of view – look in retrospect unsurprising and even inevitable. It was all 'bound to happen' once human knowledge had manifestly become too unwieldy for any one kind of professional expertise. The possibilities available included at least the following. (i) Try to cling on to a stake in the expanding natural sciences by claiming philosophy to be the most 'general' science of all. (This lets the philosopher off such hooks as having to know anything up-to-date about earthworms, outer space or genes.) (ii) Realize that (i) is a desperate pretence and go for promoting philosophy as a non-science, but one which is actually essential to effective scientific practice, i.e. the analysis of concepts underlying not only scientific thinking but thinking generally. (iii) Realizing that (ii) might entail competition with psychology, and hence precipitate a leap from the philosophical frying-pan into the empirical fire, opt for declaring philosophy warden of a timeless domain of thought which somehow exists independently of human thinkers. (iv) Recognize that there is no plausible way of proceeding in (iii) except via an investigation of how thought is expressed, and therefore re-jig philosophy as a critique of language.

This is one (but not the only) possible sketch of the background leading up to the contemporary philosophical emphasis on language. The term 'critique' of language, at least, was well chosen. If understood as an investigation of the scope and limits of language, it let the philosopher off doing any linguistic fieldwork and thus avoided the analogous trap under (ii), which might require the sage to don a white coat and make an appearance in the psychological laboratory (the first of which had been set up in Leipzig by Wundt in 1879).

Why it should fall to the philosopher to deliver a critique of language rather than to the linguist was always a more puzzling question – at least from a linguist's perspective.

The foregoing will have to serve in lieu of explanation to any reader curious enough to ask why this book has avoided, except in quotations or scare quotes, such terms as *philosophy of language* and *philosophy of linguistics.*[5] These are terms already laden with assumptions about the historical rearguard action mentioned above.

As a minor detail of intellectual history, it is perhaps worth drawing attention to the fact that this solution to philosophy's problems runs more or less parallel to the solution adopted for rhetoric (another traditional discipline which found itself facing redundancy after the Renaissance). Critical theory, a general 'critique of literature' or of public discourse in its entirety, is the eventual academic successor to rhetoric, just as a 'critique of language' in the end takes over from medieval philosophy. (The distinction between a critique of language and a critique of public discourse becomes hazy, to say the least. Hence the failure on the part of some continental writers to distinguish the two.)

What exactly hinges on this notion of a *critique*? Again, the cynical view is that you take it as implying whatever you wish. But clearly it can be taken in such a way that all the linguistic investigation involved can safely be done from the depths of an armchair. That was the position from which twentieth-century philosophers, whether or not they accepted the view that philosophy

---

[5]   On the latter, see R. Harris, 'What is philosophy of linguistics?', in R. Harré and R. Harris (eds.), *Linguistics and Philosophy. The Controversial Interface*, Oxford, Pergamon, 1993, pp. 1–19.

was a critique of language, – Moore, Russell, Wittgenstein, Carnap, Quine, *et al.* – did whatever linguistic research they needed. They may have looked up dictionaries occasionally, but that was as near as they ever got to investigating linguistic 'facts'.

Some would argue that even if the great majority of modern 'linguistic philosophers' were guilty of doing armchair linguistics (and not very well researched armchair linguistics, to boot), an honourable exception nevertheless has to be made in favour of J. L. Austin. He, we are told, advocated linguistic research by controlled stages, involving

> a team of a dozen or so working together; the members supplemented each other and corrected each other's oversights and errors. Having collected its terms and idioms, the group must proceed to the second stage in which, by telling circumstantial stories and conducting dialogues, they give as clear and detailed examples as possible of circumstances under which this idiom is to be preferred to that, and that to this, and of where we should (do) use this term and where that.[6]

The great merit of this method was alleged to be that – in contrast to the crude sociological procedure of research by questionnaire –

> Experience shows that a group, not just a group of Oxford philosophers but, say, a mixed American and British group, can reach virtual unanimity on these matters.[7]

[6] J. O. Urmson, 'A symposium on Austin's method', in K. T. Fann (ed.), *Symposium on J. L. Austin*, London, Routledge & Kegan Paul, 1969, p. 79.

[7] Urmson, *loc. cit.*

The sceptical linguist, who had seen decades of in-house fighting about 'discovery procedures', 'sampling' and 'linguistic corpora', might well have been forgiven for collapsing in hysterical laughter on hearing this solemn and grotesque little methodological proposal from an Oxford philosopher. Here, evidently, was the result *not* of linguistics entering into competition with philosophy but of philosophy setting up in competition with linguistics!

*   *   *

One suspects that linguistics began to claim the attention of philosophers only when the latter were challenged not on issues of methodology or 'data collection', but on the more visceral issue of what constituted a linguistic 'theory'.

In the early 1950s, Quine had been more or less overtly contemptuous of linguistic semantics. He wrote:

> Lexicography is concerned, or seems to be concerned, with identification of meanings, and the investigation of semantic change is concerned with change of meaning. Pending a satisfactory explanation of the notion of meaning, linguists in semantic fields are in the situation of not knowing what they are talking about.[8]

For a linguist, this might easily be taken as implying that for enlightenment on such matters, one should look not to linguistics but to philosophy. That interpretation might seem to be confirmed by Quine's immediately following remarks:

[8]   W. V. O. Quine, 'The problem of meaning in linguistics', in W. V. O. Quine, *From a Logical Point of View*, Cambridge, Mass., Harvard University Press, 1953, p. 47.

This [sc. not knowing what you are talking about in linguistics] is not an untenable situation. Ancient astronomers knew the movements of the planets remarkably well without knowing what sort of things the planets were. But it is a theoretically unsatis-factory situation, as the more theoretically minded among linguists are painfully aware.[9]

It is possible to read into this an allusion to or an endorsement of Bloomfield's capitulation to behaviourism. Leonard Bloomfield, the leading linguistic theorist of his generation, had conceded that a linguist cannot tell you the meaning of a term unless – and until – the science under which that term falls has determined the nature of the corresponding object. Thus we know what the word *salt* means, but not what the word *love* means.[10]

The many questions this raises cannot be pursued here. The point is, rather, that *within the decade* philosophers were visibly embarrassed because they themselves did not have a viable semantic theory (or a theory of syntax either). And the only people who looked likely to come up with one (or both) were linguists. J. R. Searle, commenting on Austin's approach to language, confessed:

Without any coherent general theory of syntax and semantics on which to base particular linguistic analyses, the philosopher who looks to the so-called use of expressions has no way of distinguishing features of utterances which are due to particular words from features which are due to other factors,

[9] *Ibid.*, p. 47.

[10] L. Bloomfield, *Language*, London, Allen & Unwin, 1935, p. 139.

such as the syntactical character of the sentence or the type of speech act being performed.[11]

In 1962, in a paper entitled 'What's wrong with the philosophy of language?', J. Fodor and J. J. Katz answered their own question by pointing out that what it lacked was precisely the systematic and comprehensive characterization of the native speaker's linguistic abilities which a formal generative linguistic theory could now provide.[12]

But how, exactly, might this improve philosophical analyses? Zeno Vendler provided an example in *The Journal of Philosophy* for 1965:

> Had Austin known transformational grammar, he would not have been misled into assimilating facts to events by the possibility of saying, for instance, both that the collapse of the Germans is an event and that the collapse of the Germans is a fact. For he would have realized that the phrase "the collapse of the Germans" is transformationally ambiguous ...[13]

Whether the example was important or even plausible was hardly the point. The philosopher's bluff had been called. Quine's criticism of linguistics for its theoretical inadequacies ten years earlier had rebounded on his own discipline.

What was to be done? Anyone who reads the academic journals of the period can see how philosophers turned with relief towards the new light shining

---

[11] J. R. Searle, 'Assertions and aberrations', *Inquiry*, vol. I, 1958, pp. 172–212.

[12] J. Fodor and J. J. Katz, 'What's wrong with the philosophy of language?', *The Journal of Philosophy*, vol. LIX, 1962. Reprinted in C. Lyas (ed.), *Philosophy and Linguistics*, London, Macmillan, 1971.

[13] *The Journal of Philosophy*, vol. LXII, no. 20, p. 590.

from M.I.T. as towards a star of Bethlehem. Almost overnight, the old-style linguistic philosophy was abandoned as philosophers set out for Boston to greet the new Messiah. It must have been a disappointment when they got there to discover that the Messiah's message was a retelling in new metalinguistic terminology of the old, old story about the parts of speech and the sentence.

* * *

The writer of this book has no ambition to adjudicate on past or present demarcation disputes between linguists and philosophers. But the relationship between these two groups is of interest to him for a different reason. It seems to him undeniable that this two-thousand-year-old division of linguistic inquiry between separate disciplines is itself largely responsible for the failure so far in Western culture to deliver anything like a convincing account of language or a comprehensive rationale of linguistic investigation. Paradoxically, however, this is not because of some deep division over what language is. On the contrary, it has suited all parties to accept a rather simplistic view of language, because that allows them to stake out their respective academic territories in defensible ways.

I am struck by the way in which philosophers have sometimes approached the position I am here maintaining, only to retreat at the last minute instead of taking the final step. For example, in a paper never published during his lifetime,[14] Austin acknowledged that 'there is something spurious' about the *general*

---

[14] 'The meaning of a word', in J. L. Austin, *Philosophical Papers*, ed. J. O. Urmson and G. J. Warnock, Oxford, Clarendon, 1961, pp. 23–43.

question 'What is the meaning of a word?', and described it as a 'nonsense question'. But he still did not want to treat as problematic a question like 'What is the meaning of the word *word*?'. On the contrary, he held that this could be answered in exactly the same way as 'What is the meaning of the word *cat*?'. This insistence that metalanguage has no special status is perhaps what one might expect of an 'ordinary language' philosopher. But it seems to me there is a deeper reason, which has to do only incidentally with 'ordinary language' philosophy. Austin drew back on the brink of calling into question the traditional metalanguage itself; for such a move would have left him, *qua* philosopher, with nothing to say on the subject of meaning at all. Similarly, in developing his very 'untraditional' theories of illocutionary force and performative acts, Austin took care not to disturb the old metalinguistic foundations on which those theories were built.

Here I have tried to use the question 'What do you mean by that?' as a more radical tool for linguistic inquiry. I have tried to give some indication of how, if thus used, it could expose to critical scrutiny the strategies by which both philosophy and linguistics reproduce the ways of talking about language which it is in their own interests to safeguard and promote.

The method is not without risks. It took – as one might expect – a sociologist to discover by experiment that if you persist obstinately in asking 'What do you mean by that?' people will treat you as a joker or even become hostile.[15] But the risks are worth taking if you want to find out for yourself how language works.

---

[15] J. Heritage, *Garfinkel and Ethnomethodology*, Cambridge, Polity, 1984, p. 80.

What you must remember is that as soon as you allow the question 'What do you mean by that?' to be replaced by 'What does that mean?', and treat the latter as if 'that' had a meaning independently of where and when it was said, by whom or to whom, then you are already creating metalinguistic illusions for yourself.

REFERENCES

Aristotle, *Categories, On Interpretation*, trans. H. P. Cooke, Loeb Classical Library, London, Heinemann, 1938.

Augustine, *Confessions*, trans. W. Watts, Loeb Classical Library, London, Heinemann, 1912.

Auroux, S., *La Révolution technique de la grammatisation*, Liège, Mardaga, 1994.

Austin, J. L., *Philosophical Papers*, ed. J. O. Urmson and G. J. Warnock, Oxford, Clarendon, 1961.

Ayer, A. J., *Thinking and Meaning*, London, Lewis, 1947.

Bach, E., *An Introduction to Transformational Grammars*, New York, Holt, Rinehart & Winston, 1964.

Bacon, F., *The Physical and Metaphysical Works of Lord Bacon*, trans. J. Devey, London, 1853.

Bloomfield, L., *Language*, London, Allen & Unwin, 1935.

Calame-Griaule, G., *Ethnologie et langage. La parole chez les Dogon*, 2nd ed., Paris, Institut d'Ethnologie, 1987.

Carnap, R., *The Logical Syntax of Language*, trans. A. Smeaton, London, Kegan Paul, Trench, Trubner & Co., 1937.

183

Chomsky, N., *Rules and Representations*, Oxford, Blackwell, 1980.

Crystal, D., *Introduction to Linguistic Pathology*, London, Arnold, 1980.

—— *Encyclopedic Dictionary of Language and Languages*, Oxford, Blackwell, 1992.

Denes, P. B. and E. N. Pinson, *The Speech Chain*, Garden City, N.Y., Anchor, 1963.

Eaton, R. M., *General Logic*, London, Scribner, 1931.

Edwards, P. (ed.), *The Encyclopedia of Philosophy*, New York, Macmillan, 1967.

Flew, A. G. N. (ed.), *Logic and Language*, Oxford, Blackwell, 1951.

Fodor, J. A., *The Language of Thought*, New York, Crowell, 1975.

Fodor, J. A. and Katz, J. J., 'What's wrong with the philosophy of language?', *The Journal of Philosophy*, vol. LIX, 1962.

Fung, Y–L., *A Short History of Chinese Philosophy*, ed. D. Bodde, New York, Free Press, 1948.

—— *A History of Chinese Philosophy*, trans. D. Bodde, 2nd ed., Princeton, Princeton University Press, 1952.

Gombert, J. E., *Metalinguistic Development*, Chicago, University of Chicago Press, 1992.

Harris, R., *The Language-Makers*, London, Duckworth, 1980.

—— 'What is philosophy of linguistics?', in R. Harré and R. Harris (eds.), *Linguistics and Philosophy. The*

Controversial Interface, Oxford, Pergamon, 1993, pp. 1–19.

Harris, Z. S., *Structural Linguistics*, Chicago, University of Chicago Press, 1951.

—— 'Distributional structure', *Word*, vol. 10, no. 2/3, 1954, pp. 146–62.

Heritage, J., *Garfinkel and Ethnomethodology*, Cambridge, Polity, 1984.

Hobbes, T., *Leviathan*, [1651], London, Dent, 1914.

Hockett, C. F., *A Course in Modern Linguistics*, New York, Macmillan, 1956.

Hume, D., *Enquiries concerning Human Understanding and concerning the Principles of Morals*, [1777], ed. P. H. Nidditch, 3rd ed., Oxford, Clarendon, 1975.

Keller, H., *The Story of My Life*, Garden City, Doubleday & Doran, 1902.

Kneale, W. and M. Kneale, *The Development of Logic*, rev. ed., Oxford, Clarendon, 1984.

Lallot, J., *La Grammaire de Denys le Thrace*, Paris, CNRS, 1989.

Locke, J., *An Essay concerning Human Understanding*, [1706], ed. A. C. Fraser, repr. New York, Dover, 1959.

Lyas, C. (ed.), *Philosophy and Linguistics*, London, Macmillan, 1971.

Lyons, J., *Introduction to Theoretical Linguistics*, Cambridge, Cambridge University Press, 1968.

—— *Linguistic Semantics: An Introduction*, Cambridge, Cambridge University Press, 1995.

Mehta, V., *Fly and the Fly-Bottle. Encounters with British Intellectuals*, Harmondsworth, Penguin, 1965.

Moulton, W. G., *A Linguistic Guide to Language Learning*, 2nd ed., Modern Language Association of America, 1970.

Peirce, C. S., *Collected Papers*, vols. 1–6 ed. C. Hartshorne and P. Weiss, vols. 7–8 ed. A. Burks, Cambridge, Mass., Harvard University Press, 1931–58.

Plato, *Cratylus*, trans. H. N. Fowler, Loeb Classical Library, London, Heinemann, 1926.

Quine, W. V. O., *From a Logical Point of View*, Cambridge, Mass., Harvard University Press, 1953.

———— *Elementary Logic*, rev. ed., Cambridge, Mass., Harvard University Press, 1966.

Rorty, R., *Philosophy and the Mirror of Nature*, Princeton, Princeton University Press, 1979.

Saussure, F. de, *Course in General Linguistics*, trans. R. Harris, London, Duckworth, 1983.

Searle, J. R., 'Assertions and aberrations', *Inquiry*, vol. 1, 1958, pp. 172–212.

Sextus Empiricus, *Adversus Mathematicos*, trans. R. G. Bury, Loeb Classical Library, London, Heinemann, 1949.

Sinclair, W. A., *The Traditional Formal Logic*, London, Methuen, 1937.

Strawson, P. F., 'Construction and analysis', in A. J. Ayer *et al.*, *The Revolution in Philosophy*, London, Macmillan, 1956, pp. 97–110.

—— 'Meaning, truth and communication', in N. Minnis (ed.), *Linguistics at Large*, St. Albans, Picador, 1973, pp. 89–110.

Tarski, A., 'The semantic conception of truth', *Philosophy and Phenomenological Research*, vol. 4, 1944, pp. 341–75. Reprinted in L. Linsky (ed.), *Semantics and the Philosophy of Language*, Urbana, University of Illinois Press, 1952.

Thucydides, *History of the Peloponnesian War*, trans. R. Warner, rev. ed., London, Penguin, 1972.

Urmson, J. O., 'A symposium on Austin's method', in K. T. Fann (ed.), *Symposium on J. L. Austin*, London, Routledge & Kegan Paul, 1969.

Wittgenstein, L., *Tractatus Logico-Philosophicus*, London, Routledge & Kegan Paul, 1922.

—— *Philosophical Investigations*, trans. G. E. M. Anscombe, 2nd ed., Oxford, Blackwell, 1958.

INDEX

NOTES